COME AND SEE

Catholic Bible Study

Prophets and Apostles

by

Fr. Joseph Ponessa, S.S.D

and

Laurie Watson Manhardt, Ph.D.

1

Emmaus Road Publishing
827 North Fourth Street
Steubenville, Ohio 43952

All rights reserved. Published 2004
Printed in the United States of America
Third impression 2012

Library of Congress Control Number: 2004106420
ISBN 1931018197

Unless otherwise indicated, Scripture quotations are taken
from the Catholic Edition of the Revised Standard Version of the Bible,
copyright 1965, 1966 by the Division of Christian Education of the
National Council of the Churches of Christ in the
United States of America. Used by permission.
All rights reserved.

Excerpts from the English translation of the
Catechism of the Catholic Church for the United States of America
copyright 1994, United States Catholic Conference, Inc.
—Libreria Editrice Vaticana.
English translation of the *Catechism of the Catholic Church:
Modifications from the Editio Typica* copyright 1997,
United States Catholic Conference, Inc.
—Libreria Editrice Vaticana. Cited in the text as *"Catechism."*

Cover design and layout by
Jacinta Calcut/Image Graphics and Design

Cover artwork:
Pietro Cavallini, *Last Judgment*

Nihil obstat: Rev. Joseph N. Rosie, *Censor Librorum*
Imprimatur: ✠ John M. Smith
Bishop of Trenton
May 1, 2004

The *nihil obstat* and *imprimatur* are official declarations
that a book or pamphlet is free of doctrinal or moral error.
No implication is contained therein that those who have
granted the *nihil obstat* and *imprimatur* agree with
the contents, opinions, or statements expressed.

For additional information on the "Come and See"
Catholic Bible study series visit www. Catholicbiblestudy.net

Copyright ©2004 by Fr. Joseph Ponessa and Laurie Manhardt

Catholic Bible Study
Prophets and Apostles

INTRODUCTION

"Thy words were found, and I ate them,
and thy words became to me a joy and the delight of my heart."
JEREMIAH 15:16

May God set His Word in your heart
and fill you with everlasting joy.

May you walk in His ways,
always knowing what is right and good,
until you enter your heavenly inheritance. Amen.

God bless you as you embark upon this ***Come and See: Catholic Bible Study ~ Prophets and Apostles***. Whether you have studied Sacred Scripture for many years or are opening the Word of God for the first time, trust that your efforts will be pleasing to God and prove to be rewarding for you as well.

God's Word enables you to study again and again and receive new insights and fresh understanding. If you are a beginner to Bible study, the Holy Spirit can give you insights that will astound you and also bless the veterans in your group. If you are a seasoned student of God's Word, you know that God always has more. Share what God gives you and expect to be surprised with even more blessings from Him through others in your group. Studying Scripture with others multiplies the possibilities of receiving fresh insights and blessings, as well as storing God's Word deep in your heart.

What you need!

To do this Bible Study, you need a Catholic Bible, and a ***Catechism of the Catholic Church (CCC)***. When choosing a Bible, recall that the Catholic Bible contains 73 books, compared with others having only 66 books. The additional seven books from the Hebrew Scriptures, called Old Testament books, and extra chapters of Daniel provide inspiring passages that you will need to consult. If you find Sirach and Tobit in your Bible table of contents, you have a complete Catholic bible. ***The Council of Hippo approved these 73 books in 393 AD,*** and this has remained the official canon of Sacred Scripture since the 4th century. The Council of Trent authoritatively reaffirmed these books of the Bible in 1545 AD.

For Bible Study purposes, choose a word-for-word, literal translation rather than a paraphrase. Some excellent translations for Bible study are the Revised Standard Version (RSV-CE) 1965, 1966, the Jerusalem Bible (JB) 1966, and the New American Bible (NAB) 1970. Another option is the Douay-Rheims (DR) Bible, which was completed in 1609 AD. The Good News Bible, or Today's English Version (TEV), 1976 represents a paraphrase of the Bible, which will be difficult to use in this type of formal Bible study.

Browse in a Catholic book store to determine which translation reads best for you. Compare Psalm 1 in several translations before making your selection. Do you sense that Psalm 1 is preparing you to recognize Jesus, the righteous, blessed man who will save the world? Does the translation of Psalm 1 inspire you to want to emulate that Righteous One and walk in His ways? The entirety of the Old Testament points to Jesus, the Father's provision for the atonement of sin. The New Testament reveals God the Father through Jesus Christ in the power of the Holy Spirit. Choose a translation that makes the mystery of God come alive for you. Often an old Bible proves to be a precious treasure.

Seek a quiet place for prayer and study. Adoration of the Blessed Sacrament in a chapel near your home may enable you to do some Bible study in the presence of Our Lord. Set aside time to pray and study God's Word. *1) Pray, 2) Read the Bible chapters and commentary and then 3) Write answers to the questions using the Bible and Catechism.* This year, you will read several small books of the Bible from both the prophets of the Hebrew Scriptures *(Old Testament)* and the New Testament apostles. You will see for yourself how God's promises are fulfilled in the New Covenant. You may want to get some Bible Tabs to help you move back and forth through these books quickly and easily.

Please, share aloud with your small group members only on those questions for which you have written answers!

Getting Started

- *Pray to the Holy Spirit.* Ask God for wisdom on when to have the Bible study, whom to study with and when and where to meet.
- *Invite neighbors and friends* to a "Get Acquainted Coffee" and find out who will make a commitment to meet for 60-90 minutes once a week for group Bible Study.
- *Determine a day of the week and time of day* to meet. For mothers and children, one morning from 9:30-11:00 might be best, or an afternoon from 1:00-2:30 pm. Working people may be well served in the evening from 7:30-9:00 pm. It may be impossible to find a perfect time for everyone, so go with what seems to work best.
- *Find an appropriate location.* Start in someone's home and then, as your group becomes larger, ask the pastor of your parish if you could meet in church or school facilities. Pray beforehand and offer this book to him for his review and approval.
- *Explore the possibility of hiring a baby-sitter* for young mothers and share the cost among everyone, or investigate whether some students might do childcare for the Bible study as a project for their Confirmation service requirement.
- *Consider a Cooperative Arrangement* in which women take turns caring for and teaching the young children. All women, even grandmothers and women without children, should take turns to serve the little children as an offering to God.
- *Gather a small prayer group to pray regularly for your Bible study* and for your specific needs and challenges. Pray to discern God's will, brainstorm and make plans.

Pray that God will anoint specific people to lead your study. Faithful, practicing Catholics are needed to fill the following positions:

- **Teachers** ~ take overall responsibility to read commentaries and prepare a 20-30 minute wrap-up lecture after the small group discussions each week.
- **Song Leaders** ~ plan and lead a short hymn that everyone can sing to start the Bible study each week.
- **Prayer Leaders** ~ begin with a prayer and ask someone to prepare a short five minute opening devotional each week. This could be an answer to prayer or personal testimony.
- **Children's Leaders** ~ hire babysitters, prepare lessons and teach pre-school children who attend Bible Study with their mothers.
- **Coordinators** ~ communicate with parish personnel about needs for space and use of facilities. Put invitations in church bulletins. Make sure rooms are left in good condition.

Small group facilitators will be needed for each small group. Try to enlist two mature Catholics who are good listeners to serve together as small group leaders for each group. Small group facilitators must be practicing Catholics and share the following responsibilities for their small discussion group:

- Pray for each member of your small group each day.
- Make a name tag for each member of the group.
- Meet before the study to pray with other leaders.
- Discuss all the questions in the lesson each week.
- Begin and end on time

- Make sure that each person in the group shares each week. Ask each person to read a question and have the first chance to answer it.
- You might just go around in a circle, so that each person can look forward to his or her turn. After reading the question others should feel free to offer answers as well.
- Ensure that no one person dominates the discussion, including you!
- Keep the discussion positive and focused on this week's lesson.
- Speak kindly and charitably. Steer conversation away from any negative or uncharitable speech, gossip or griping. Don't badmouth anyone, any group or any church.

- Listen well! Keep your eyes and ears open. Give your full attention to the one speaking.
- Look at people while they are speaking. Get comfortable with silence and pauses in the discussion. Be patient. Encourage quieter people to share first. Ask questions.
- If questions, misunderstandings or disagreements arise, refer them to the question box for a teacher or the parish priest to research and discuss later.
- Arrange for a social activity each month.

Invite your pastor, associate, visiting priests and religious to participate in the Bible study. Ask for their blessings. Invite them to come and pray with the Bible study members. See if they would like to come and answer some written questions from the question box periodically. Accept whatever they can offer to the Bible study. However, don't *expect* anything from them. Appreciate that the priests may be very busy, and don't add additional burdens.

If a priest offers to give a devotional or closing lecture, accept with gratitude.

---

† Jesus chose a group of twelve apostles. So, perhaps small groups should be about twelve or thirteen people. When you get too big, break up into two groups.

† Women share best with women and men with men. If you plan a mixed Bible study, organize separate men's groups, led by men and women's groups, led by women. In a mixed group, some people may be uncomfortable sharing and sit silently.

† Offer a married couples' group if two married couples are willing to act as small group facilitators and come together to every class meeting. Each person should have his or her own book and share on his or her own home study answers.

† You may also want to consider a nursing mothers' group in which mothers can bring their infants with them and hold the babies while they share their home study work.

† A group of teenagers or young adult group could be facilitated by the parish priest or by a young adult leader.

† Family groups can work together on the home study questions on a given night of the week, with older children or parents helping younger children to find the passages in the Bible and the *Catechism*.

† Share the overall goal that *each person* in each group shares aloud each time the group meets. Everyone should contribute every time the Bible study meets!

† Sit next to the most talkative person in the group and across from the quietest. Use eye contact to encourage quiet members to speak up. Serve everyone and hear from everyone. Listening in Bible study is just as important as talking! Evaluate each week, "Am I a good listener? Did I really hear what others shared? Was I attentive or distracted? Did I affirm others? Did I talk too much?"

Social Activities

God has created us as social creatures, needing to relate communally. Large churches present challenges for parishioners to get to know one another. Some people belong to a parish for years without getting to know others. Newcomers may never get noticed and welcomed. Bible Study offers an opportunity for spiritual nourishment as well as inclusion and hospitality.

Occasional social activities are offered in this book. These socials are simple, fun and non-threatening. In planning your social activities, be a good sport, try to attend and share with your small group. Keep in mind the following when planning:

※ Agree on a time when most of the group can meet. This could be right before or after the Bible study or on a different day of the week, perhaps even Saturday morning.

※ Invite people to come to your home for the social time. Jesus was comfortable visiting in the homes of the rich and the poor. So whether you live in a small apartment or a big mansion, as a Christian you can offer hospitality to those God sends along your way.

"Do not neglect to show hospitality to strangers,
for thereby some have entertained angels unawares" *(Hebrews 13:2).*

※ Keep it simple! Just a beverage and cookies work well. Simplicity blesses others. People can squeeze together on a sofa or stand around the kitchen. The important thing is to offer hospitality and love one another as Jesus directed. Don't fuss.

※ Help out the group leader. If the Bible study meets in someone else's home, invite the group to come to your place for the social time. Don't make the group leader do it all. Jump right in and offer. Be a blessing to others.

※ If your Bible study meets in church, do not fall into the convenience of staying at the church for socials. You might have to drive a distance to someone's home, but it may be the first time anyone from the parish has taken the trouble to come out to their home to visit. Trust God. It's worth it. God will bless your efforts at offering hospitality to your Bible study group and also your efforts in accepting the hospitality of others.

Consider the following times for your socials.

9:30 a.m. - 10:30 a.m.	Saturday coffee	11:30 a.m. - 12:30 p.m.	Luncheon
3:00 p.m. - 4:00 p.m.	Afternoon tea	8:00 p.m. - 9:00 p.m.	Dessert

Modify times to meet your specific needs. If the parish has Saturday morning Mass at 8:00 a.m., adjust the time of your social to accommodate those members of your group who would like to attend Mass and need some travel time to get to the social. If lunch after the Bible study makes too long of a day for mothers with children, plan the social for another day. A mothers' group might meet after school when high school students can baby-sit.

Practical Schedule

Take responsibility for being a good steward of time. God gives each of us twenty-four hours a day. If the Bible study becomes loose, busy people may drop out. Late starts encourage tardiness and punish the prompt. Be a good steward of time. Begin and end each Bible study with prayer at the agreed upon time.

If many people consistently arrive late, investigate whether you have chosen the best time, and pray for God's wisdom to determine the best time for most members. If people leave early, check if you have a conflict with the kindergarten or bus schedule. Perhaps beginning a few minutes earlier or later could serve those who need to pick up children.

Suggested Bible Study Class Schedules

Morning Class

9:30 a.m.	Welcome, Song, Prayer
9:50 a.m.	Small Group Discussion
10:30 a.m.	Wrap-up Lecture
11:00 a.m.	Closing Prayer

Evening Class

7:30 p.m.	Welcome, Song, Prayer
7:50 p.m.	Small Group Discussion
8:30 p.m.	Wrap-up Lecture
9:00 p.m.	Closing Prayer

Afternoon Class

1:00 p.m.	Welcome, Song, Prayer
1:20 p.m.	Small Group Discussion
2:00 p.m.	Wrap-up Lecture
2:30 p.m.	Closing Prayer

Always begin and end with prayer!

Wrap-Up Lecture

1) A closing, wrap-up lecture may be presented for your group.
2) Or simply share on the home study questions and close with prayer.

When using a closing lecture, the teacher spends extra time in prayer and study over the passages of Scripture studied and consults several Bible Study Commentaries. Several members of the Bible Study Leaders' Group could serve in taking turns to prepare the wrap-up lectures. Invite priests, deacons and religious sisters to give an occasional lecture.

The Lecturer's Responsibilities include the following:

- Be a faithful, practicing Catholic. Seek out spiritual direction. Receive the Sacrament of Reconciliation frequently.
- Obtain the approval and blessing of your parish priest to teach.
- Use several different lecturers, whenever possible.
- Pray daily for all the leaders and members of the study.
- Pray over the lesson to be studied.

- Outline the Bible chapters to be discussed.
- Identify the main idea of the Bible study lesson.
- Find a personal application from the passages studied. The personal application suggests what one can do to respond to God's Word.
- Plan a wrap-up lecture with a beginning, a middle and an end.
- Use index card or notes to keep you focused. Don't read your lecture! Talk to people. Most folks can read.

- Proclaim, teach and reiterate the teachings of the Catholic Church. Learn what the Catholic Church teaches and proclaim the fullness of truth.
- Illustrate the main idea presented in the passage by using true stories from the lives of contemporary Christians or from lives of the saints.
- Use visuals ~ a flip chart or overhead transparencies if possible.
- Plan a skit, act out a Bible story and interact with the group.

- Provide a question box. Find answers to difficult questions or ask a parish priest to come and discuss some questions from the question box.
- When difficult or complex personal problems arise or are shared in the group, seek out the counsel of a priest.
- Begin and end on time. When you get to the end of your talk, stop and pray.

Begin with prayer. End with prayer.

Challenges

Any group can attract people with problems and difficulties. Don't try to be all things for all people. When problems arise, direct them to a priest. Try to be faithful in this one thing.

St. Paul advises, "Speak the truth in love . . . be kind to one another, tenderhearted, forgiving one another, as God in Christ forgave you" (Ephesians 4:15, 32).

"All scripture is inspired by God and profitable for teaching, for reproof, for correction, and for training in righteousness, that the man of God may be complete, equipped for every good work" (2 Timothy 3:16-17).

"If you want to be always in God's company, you must pray regularly and read regularly. *When we pray, we talk to God; when we read, God talks to us.* All spiritual growth comes from reading and reflection. By reading we learn what we did not know; by reflection we retain what we have learned.

Reading the holy Scriptures confers two benefits. It trains the mind to understand them; it turns attention from the follies of the world and leads to the love of God. First learn how the Scriptures are to be understood, and then see how to expound them with profit and in a manner worthy of them. A man must first be eager to understand what he is reading before he is fit to proclaim what he has learned.

The conscientious reader will be more concerned to carry out what he has read than merely to acquire knowledge of it. For it is a less serious fault to be ignorant of an objective than it is to fail to carry out what we do know. In reading we aim at knowing, but we must put into practice what we have learned in our course of study. The more you devote yourself to a study of the sacred utterances, the richer will be your understanding of them, just as the more the soil is tilled, the richer the harvest.

Learning unsupported by grace may get into our ears; but it never reaches the heart. But when God's grace touches our innermost minds to bring understanding, His word which has been received by the ear sinks deep into the heart."

St. Isidore, Bishop and Doctor, (560-636 AD), *Book of Maxims, 3. 8-10.*

Begin this study of the Prophets and Apostles in expectant faith, hope, charity and prayer.

Come Holy Spirit, open my mind and my heart.
Enlighten me, apply Your Word to my life and use it to transform me.
Make me a good listener. Draw me closer to You, my God

1, 2, & 3 JOHN
Apostle of Love

Memory Verse

**"God is love, and he who abides in love abides in God,
and God abides in him."**

1 JOHN 4:16B

Meet John. Through the pages of this book, you will encounter the writing of sixteen friends of God, eleven prophets and five apostles. Of these, the one closest to the heart of Christ was John, under whose name the New Testament presents some of its most sublime writings—a Gospel, three letters and the Book of Revelation.

The First Letter of John begins in the first person plural, "we," but the author is clearly one person. The letter never names its own author, but it belongs to the same world of thought and expression as the Gospel. These works display an insight into the Person and Mind of Christ that only the closest of friends could know.

Many scholars have speculated that the beloved apostle is not the same person as the Evangelist, or that the Evangelist is not the same person as the author of the letter. Such speculation may have had some justification when it was believed that the Johannine writings could be dated as much as 150 years after the death of Christ. However, discovery in Egypt of a papyrus datable to 125 AD containing a fragment of the Gospel has squashed the late composition theory, and pulled the rug out from under the hypothesis that a later Gentile wrote the works ascribed to John.

Therefore, we do not need to apologize for adhering to the ancient tradition that the author of this letter is none other than Yohannan ben-Zebedee (John, the son of Zebedee), the youngest of the apostles, who was called from his father's fishing boat at a very tender age to witness the greatest Life of all time and of eternity.

In Hebrew, the original name reads *Yo-Hannan*. The first element of the name, *Yo* is an abbreviation of the Divine Name, the so-called Tetragrammaton, which contains the four consonants YHWH. This element appears in many Hebrew names and words, sometimes at the beginning as here, and sometimes at the end, as in *Hallelu-Yah* ("Praise the LORD"). Another person appears in the pages of the Bible with a variation on this name, with the elements reversed; that person is Hananiah (Daniel 1:7), or *Hannan-Ya*. This means the same thing as *Yo-Hannan*, but with the two parts of it switched.

The name *Yo-Hannan* or *Hannan-Ya* means, "The Lord loves," or "The Lord is love." Thus the theme "God is love," found in both the Gospel of St. John and the First Letter of John, is a kind of midrashic expansion or commentary upon the human author's name. Also, when the author of the Gospel calls himself "the beloved apostle," this is coded language signifying John, whose name means love.

What is an apostle? The very first paragraph of 1 John gives an excellent description of what constitutes an apostle of the Lord: *someone who has heard, has seen with his own eyes, has looked upon and touched with his own hands the Word of Life,* and then goes on to testify and proclaim this to us, so that we may have fellowship with him. There are two aspects to this definition of apostleship: first the eye-witness experience, and second the giving of testimony. The eye-witness experience looks back to Christ's appearance in history, while the testimony looks forward to present and future generations and ultimately to the second coming of Christ at the end of history.

The whole Church through all time depends upon the testimony of those who knew the Lord Jesus in person, who heard Him preach, who saw Him work miracles, and above all saw Him crucified and risen. *Only one person meets every one of those characteristics perfectly, and that is John, because he was the only apostle who followed Jesus to the foot of the Cross and watched the Passion transpire before his very eyes.* Paul was an apostle only in an extended sense, because he meets none of the criteria here in a perfect way; Paul was an apostle the way bishops today are apostles, by succession to the apostles. Paul and bishops today testify not to what they personally have seen, but to what the apostles before them saw. There is a succession of testimony, but there was only one generation that was privileged to have the eye-witness experience. All succeeding generations are dependent upon them. That is why we affirm in the Nicene Creed that we believe in "One, holy, catholic and apostolic Church." Any church which proclaims a testimony other than the one proclaimed by the first apostles could not be the same church founded upon the apostles.

While bishops today do not have a personal experience of the historical Christ, they need to base their testimony, as St. Paul did, upon their own spiritual experience of the living Christ. Their personal experience cannot rise to the same level as the eye-witness experience of John and the others, but it can and must form the basis of their faith and their zealous witness to the reality of Jesus Christ yesterday, today and forever.

The Goodness of God ~ An important theme of the Johannine writings is the absolute goodness of God. John writes in this letter, "God is light and in Him there is no darkness" (1 John 1:5). With this statement, John condemns the errors of Manichaeism, a popular religious movement originating in Persia. The pre-Zoroastrian Persians believed in two gods, a god of goodness and a god of evil. The two gods were supposedly in combat with each other, and human beings were caught in the middle between them. The Manichaeans saw a world of light and darkness, both of which had absolute and divine qualities. While John draws upon the images of light and darkness, he takes care to dissociate himself from the theological errors of those who viewed darkness as a quality of the divine. For John, darkness is not the equal of light but only the absence of light.

John teaches clearly that God is all-good. No distinction exists between the goodness and the power of God. *Everything God does is motivated by pure love.* The divine positive will commands only good things; the divine permissive will allows evil to exist for some purpose not fully known to us, such as human freedom. The power of God can bring good out of evil, and thus can make all things work for the good. The mere existence of evil is no obstacle to our faith in the absolute goodness of God. John experienced this absolute goodness in the Person of Jesus Christ, and while he had seen the greatest evil of all time take place before his very eyes in the crucifixion of Jesus, this was no stumbling-block but indeed a proof for his affirmation of the ultimate goodness of God.

The Commandment of Love—Old or New? John starts out saying in verse 7 that he is not writing a new commandment, but an old one. Then in verse 8 he reverses himself and says that the commandment really is new. Which is it, then, old or new? The rhetorical technique at work here is a figure of speech called "self-correction." A writer may make a simple statement that looks true at first glance, and tricks us into agreeing with the platitude, but then he shows us that we were not looking deep enough and that the reality is different and maybe even the reverse of what we had taken for granted. Shakespeare gives an example of this in *Julius Caesar.* Marc Antony's "I have come not to praise Caesar but to bury him," actually ends up in praising Caesar after all.

The commandment of love is not entirely new, because several versions of it are found in the Old Testament. Jesus affirms that the greatest commandment of the law is the love of God, and the second-greatest commandment of the law is the love of neighbor. He even says that the whole law and the prophets are based upon these two commandments. At the Last Supper, however, He elevates this commandment above and beyond the whole of the old law, and says "This is My commandment, that you love one another as I have loved you" (John 15:12). Jesus does not use the adjective "new" to describe the commandment on that occasion, but John, who reports Jesus' words to us in his account, attaches the term "new" here in his first letter. The commandment of love has a new rationale that it did not have before. The love of Jesus for us becomes the positive paradigm for our behavior towards one another.

John uses Cain as the negative paradigm: "We should love one another, and not be like Cain who was of the evil one and murdered his brother" (1 John 3:11-12). As Jesus shows us how we *should* behave towards one another, Cain shows us how *not* to behave. (If John were not Jewish, why is he using an example from the Jewish scriptures? If he were Greek, wouldn't he use an example from pagan mythology instead? This Old Testament reference supports Jewish authorship.)

Note that the commandment of love is fully in accord with the Johannine teaching of God's absolute goodness. The commandment uses God's love as the basis for our behavior. If we believed in a god who was both good and evil, we would be split into two personalities, a good one and a bad one, just as our god was. Since we believe, however, in a God who is nothing but good, and has demonstrated this goodness to us in creating us and then redeeming us, we now are challenged to accord our behavior with His.

The First Letter of John contains eight or more rephrasings of this new commandment:

— he who says he abides in him ought to walk in the same way in which he walked (1 John 2:6)
— he who says he is in the light and hates his brother is in the darkness still (1 John 2:9)
— he who loves his brother abides in the light (1 John 2:10)
— he who hates his brother is in the darkness and walks in darkness (1 John 2:11)
— we should love one another and not be like Cain (1 John 3:11-12)
— love one another, just as he has commanded us (1 John 3:23)
— let us love one another; for love is of God (1 John 4:7)
— he who loves God should love his brother also (1 John 4:21)

We could read this letter and wonder why John keeps repeating himself. If this new law is to be the be-all and end-all of our religion, though, it is important for us to cast this commandment in iron and admit of no loopholes. By paraphrasing and rephrasing the commandment, John gives the legalistically minded among us no means to slip past the commandment. John states the commandment positively several ways, and he states the commandment negatively a couple of ways, like the flip side of the coin. By the time he is finished, we have no wiggle-room left. We must love one another, period.

The Three Witnesses ~ John writes that there are three witnesses—the Spirit, the water and the blood (1 John 5:8). Now Jewish law required only two witnesses, but John combines in this statement two different events told of in his Gospel.

On each occasion, the baptism and death of Jesus, there were two witnesses:
—at the baptism in the Jordan, there were two witnesses,
the Spirit (in the form of a dove) and the water;
— after the death of Jesus on the Cross, there were two witnesses,
the blood and the water that flowed from His side.

One event occurred at the beginning of Jesus' public ministry and the other at the end. The common witness to both events is the water, but it is joined by the Spirit in the case of the baptism and the blood in the case of the crucifixion. Assembling the complete testimony for Christ's ministry upon the earth, the three witnesses agree with each other. John saw all three, the Spirit, the water and the blood, and he reports to us what he has seen. The case is proven to the satisfaction of the jury: Jesus Christ is the Word of Life incarnate. The apostolic witness is about Jesus Christ, God and Man.

Eternal life is the life of God himself and at the same time the *life of the children of God*. As they ponder this unexpected and inexpressible truth which comes from God in Christ, believers cannot fail to be filled with ever new wonder and unbounded gratitude. They can say in the words of the Apostle John: "See what love the Father has given us, that we should be called children of God; and so we are . . . Beloved, we are God's children now; it does not yet appear what we shall be, but we know that when he appears we shall be like him, for we shall see him as he is" (1 John 3:1-2).

Here the Christian truth about life becomes most sublime. The dignity of this life is linked not only to its beginning, to the fact that it comes from God, but also to its final end, to its destiny of fellowship with God in knowledge and love of him. In the light of this truth St. Irenaeus qualifies and completes his praise of man: "the glory of God" is indeed, "man, living man," but "the life of man consists in the vision of God.
Pope John Paul II, *Evangelium Vitae*, (March 25, 1995), no. 38:1-2.

1. List the people and events from the following passages. Circle the one apostle present in all.

	PEOPLE	*EVENT*
Matthew 4:18-22		
Matthew 10:1-4		
Mark 14:32-33		
Luke 9:28-30		
John 19:25-27		
Acts 1:13		

2. Use the ***Catechism of the Catholic Church*** to define and explain the role of an "apostle." ***CCC 858, 860*** and ***Glossary***.

3. Read the three short letters, 1, 2 and 3 John in one sitting and then go back and count the number of times you find the word "love" and "truth."

   LOVE ___________ times   TRUTH ___________ times

4. Why was the First Letter of John written?   1 John 1:1-4

5. What would you say to someone who suggests there may be a "dark side" of God? 1 John 1:5

6. How does a sinner get forgiveness for sins?   1 John 1:6-10

7. What would you offer to a good person, who isn't aware of any personal sin?   1 John 1:8

8. How can you perfect your love for God?   1 John 2:4-6

9. Compare the following passages.

John 13:34-35	
1 John 2:7-11	
Matthew 5:23-24	
1 John 3:23-24	
1 John 4:7-8	

10. What does John say about "the world," our response to it and its duration? 1 John 2:15-17, 1 John 5:19

11. Who is the "antichrist?"   1 John 2:22-23

12. What will we be like when Jesus comes in glory?   1 John 3:1-3

13. Who tries to get believers to sin and how does he do it?   1 John 3:4-10

14. What admonition does John give in 1 John 3:17-18?

15. What comfort can you find in 1 John 4:4?

16. Describe the three Persons of the Blessed Trinity as found in 1 John 4:13-14.

17. What assurance could an anxious, fearful person find in 1 John 4:16-18?

18. Explain the logic of John's statement in 1 John 4:20-21.

19. What would you say to someone who finds God's commandments burdensome?
     1 John 5:1-5

20. What three witnesses testify to the Divinity of Jesus Christ?   1 John 5:6-12

21. What did Jesus come to give us?

John 3:16	
John 10:10	
1 John 5:11-12	

22. What commandment is restated in 2 John 5-6?

23. What brings joy to the apostle John? 3 John 4

24. Explain the truism found in 3 John 11.

25. Share a specific time in your life when you were in need (it could have been a small thing) and someone in the body of Christ met your need and demonstrated Christ-like love.

✽ Pray for an opportunity to show an act of kindness to someone in need this week. It could be as simple as offering encouragement to someone who is discouraged. Write it down below and then, if time permits, share with your small group members the way you have been faithful in showing this small act of love.

HABAKKUK
Prophet of Faith, Hope and Love

Memory Verse

**"Behold, he whose soul is not upright in him shall fail,
but, the righteous shall live by his faith."**

HABAKKUK 2:4

Meet Habakkuk. Verse 1 presents the human author of this short book: "The oracle of God which Habakkuk the prophet saw." "Oracle" is not an entirely precise description of this short book, for rather than an oracle of God, this book actually presents a dialogue between the prophet and God. Habakkuk proposes problems, and God responds through the course of the first two chapters. The term "saw" could also be misleading, since there are few dramatic visual images in the revelations of this book. The emphasis is on thinking rather than seeing. The philosophical dialogue about the problem of evil in the world parallels the theme of the Book of Job. Like Job, Habakkuk addresses a formal complaint to the Lord about the discrepancy between what is and what should be. Job struggles with his personal problems, while Habakkuk worries about the problems of the People of Israel. We don't learn much about the author Habakkuk from this opening verse, except his name and the title "prophet."

What is a Prophet? In Hebrew, the word for prophet is *Nabiy,* which means someone who speaks the words of the Lord. We still continue to emphasize this speaking function when we profess in the Nicene Creed, "We believe in the Holy Spirit . . . He has spoken through the prophets." There were many hundreds of prophets through the course of Israelite history, and only a few of them appear by name in the Bible, and even fewer of them are quoted or have books of their own. All prophets spoke, but only some of them wrote down what they said.

Some of the greatest prophets of the Old Testament—Eli, Samuel, Nathan, Elijah and Elisha—never wrote down any of their prophecies. Nonetheless, they had a great influence on the course of Israelite history by advising kings and admonishing the people in the name of the Lord. They were prophets of the spoken word, but not of the pen. Other prophets not only spoke but also wrote. These are called the "writing prophets." Within the Old Testament there are sixteen books written by prophets or their disciples. These books taken as a group constitute one of the three important sections of the Old Testament, which the Jews call "The Law, The Prophets and The Writings" (in Hebrew, *"Torah Nebiyim Kethubim,"* abbreviated *"Tanakh."*)

Habakkuk is one of the twelve "Minor Prophets." This does not mean that his message is less important than that of the major prophets, but only that he used fewer words to express that message. Indeed, Habakkuk had a great influence on the theology of the New Testament, and is quoted in the Acts of the Apostles, in the Letter of St. James, and in the Letters to the Romans, to the Galatians and to the Hebrews. This can only mean that the Book of Habakkuk was an important document to the apostles themselves (three of whom quote it) and to the whole early Church.

Who is Habakkuk? We know nothing about the personal biography of the prophet Habakkuk. From the themes of his book, nearly everyone assumes that he lived in the time of Jeremiah, shortly before the destruction of Jerusalem in 587 BC. Apparently he knew how to read and write, for he is commanded to write down his prophecies in chapter 2, verse 2: "And the LORD answered me; 'Write the vision, make it plain upon tablets.'" This seems to indicate that the Book of Habakkuk, or a large part of it, is the work of the prophet's own pen, and not that of his disciples or of some other editor. Indeed, the book begins and ends with Habakkuk's words, and not the direct words of God, so the stamp of the prophet himself is upon the whole book from start to finish.

The order to write the vision down upon tablets rather than upon paper (as in the scrolls mentioned in several other prophetic books) indicates a permanence of importance recognized from the beginning for these prophecies. The prophet believed his vision was real, and that his prophecy was intended not just for his immediate hearers, but for all future generations as well. Indeed, the mention of tablets seems to put Habakkuk's prophecy upon the same level of canonicity as the writings of Moses, who went up the mountain and brought down the tablets of the law. Since clay tablets were used more commonly in Babylon, which lies to the East of Israel, rather than in Egypt, which lies to the West, the reference to tablets here seems to indicate a strong Babylonian influence upon the culture of Israel at this time. In fact, in Habakkuk's time, the threat of destruction lay precisely from the East.

Habakkuk, Prophet of Love ~ The name *Habakkuk* means "Love's Embrace." Hence, this uncommon name, which is shared by no one else in the entire pages of Scripture, has something in common with the name "John," which means, "The Lord loves." Both names mention the theological virtue of love. The name Habakkuk sounds strange and alien to us, but to an ancient Israelite, it would be a name of deep gentleness and sensitivity.

> *We come into being upon the earth, each and every one of us, as a result of "love's embrace." Through all the days of our lives, we remain in existence because the God of love continues to hold us in the palm of His hand, in the embrace of His divine love.*

Names, so important in Hebrew psychology, and the prophetic ministry of Habakkuk offer consolation, even in the most trying of times, a reminder of our origin in love and our survival in love.

Habakkuk, Prophet of Hope ~ Indeed, Habakkuk lived in the most trying of times. It was the end of an age, when the once-glorious Kingdom of David was about to disappear from the stage of history. Already before Habakkuk's time, the nine northern tribes had been carried away into exile and had disappeared. (It is incorrect to refer to them as ten tribes, because the remaining Kingdom of Judah in the South comprised the tribes of Judah, Benjamin and much, though not all, of the tribe of Levi, the priestly tribe, who served in the Temple of Solomon in Jerusalem.) Already in Habakkuk's own time, the armies of Judah had been defeated on the field of battle, and Jerusalem stood like a ripe fruit to be plucked by the first comer.

To have a message of God's enduring love in such time means that the prophecy of Habakkuk includes a large dose of the theological virtue of hope. *Hope in good times is easy; but, hope proves its worth in times that are dangerous and unpromising.* Habakkuk and his people saw the handwriting on the wall, and knew that the end of their kingdom was coming soon. Habakkuk does not try to pull the wool over anyone's eyes, but he holds out the hope of survival for the people despite the fall of their political state.

Habakkuk, Prophet of Faith ~ Many parties in Habakkuk's time were proposing different strategies for Jewish survival. Some proposed making an alliance with the Babylonians, who were the principal threat to their existence—this would mean paying tribute to King Nebuchadnezzar, and in effect offering him the keys to the city. Others proposed making an alliance with the Pharaoh of Egypt, the other superpower in the vicinity, but this would make Judah a pawn in their regional conflicts. Others proposed the status quo, as we read in the prophet Jeremiah, presuming that God would never allow Jerusalem to fall; their slogan was "This is the temple of the LORD, the temple of the LORD, the temple of the LORD" (Jeremiah 7:4).

Habakkuk offers a clear message that differs from all these other strategies. In the course of his dialogue with the Lord, Habakkuk discovers the theological virtue of faith as the principal means whereby the people of Israel will survive. While the Israelites were on their own land, which had been given to them by the Lord, they could assume the Lord was near and live in His shadow. When they are taken into exile, they will not be able to take Him for granted any more. They will have to cling to Him by faith, and this and only this will be the means whereby their identity as a people will be assured. Hence, Habakkuk reveals in his most important verse, "[T]he righteous shall live by his faith" (Habakkuk 2:4).

Habakkuk is concerned here not just with the survival of the individual just man or woman, but with the survival of the whole people of Israel. It is a communal and historical survival that is at stake, and faith, or faithfulness, to the traditions and theology of Israel will be the one and only means for such survival. As the Psalmist says, "Some boast of chariots, and some of horses; but we boast of the name of the LORD our God. They will collapse and fall; but we shall rise and stand upright" (Psalm 20:7-8).

One of the manuscripts found in the caves of the Dead Sea in the 1950's *(The Dead Sea Scrolls)* is an ancient Jewish commentary upon the Book of Habakkuk. Here is what the ancient Jewish commentator, who lived shortly before the time of Christ and the apostles, says about Habakkuk's important teaching on survival through faith:

"But the righteous shall live by his faith. This refers to all within Judaism who carry out the Law. On account of their labor and their faith in him who expounded the Law aright, God will deliver them from the house of judgment."

Historical versus Theological Faith ~ Later, the prophecy of Habakkuk about faith will rise to a spiritual and universal level. The New Testament authors are concerned about the survival not just of a single nation upon earth but about the whole of humanity in heaven. Just as faith kept the Jewish people intact through history, faith will bring people of every nation to heaven for all eternity. St. Paul uses Habakkuk to show that all people, Jews and Gentiles alike, can achieve righteousness through faith (Romans 1:17; Habakkuk 2:4); this interpretation stands over against that of the Habakkuk commentator in two respects—universality and spirituality. The Habakkuk commentator takes Habakkuk's comment about faith in a purely national and historical sense; St. Paul takes Habakkuk's comment in a universal and spiritual sense.

Here are two divergent interpretations of Habakkuk, which are not mutually exclusive but show two levels of understanding of the impact of faith. The natural virtue of faith operates in human societies on a purely sociological level to provide a glue for human solidarity. Faithfulness makes communities strong, and any community with attributes of faithfulness will survive, whether Jewish or otherwise. That is only a this-worldly (earthly) application, however, and is not the theological gift of faith. Theological faith is meant for survival unto everlasting life, and exists for the cohesion not of worldly societies but for the cohesion of the Kingdom of God, which begins here on earth in the life of the Church Militant throughout the world, but which has no ending and will continue into the next life in the Church Suffering in purgatory and finally in the Church Triumphant in heaven. Faith brings us from one stage to the next of the church's life.

The Book of Habakkuk ends with a beautiful profession of faith which, though found in the Old Testament, is very close to the teaching of Jesus in the Sermon on the Mount. Jesus says that the poor are blessed, mourners are blessed, the persecuted are blessed. Habakkuk sees the disaster facing the people of Israel, and he looks at it straight on and finds blessing from God nonetheless. Whoever Habakkuk was, and we know so little about him, he had true grit. Like the martyrs, may we all share Habakkuk's sense of faith, which does not depend on having things go to our immediate benefit, but looks to the long term:

1. Use the ***Catechism of the Catholic Church*** or a dictionary to define "prophet."

2. Fill in the blanks from **CCC 64.**

Through the _______________, God forms his people in the _______________ of _______________, in the expectation of a_________and___________________ _________________________ intended for all, to be written on their _______________. The_______________ proclaim a radical ___________________ of the People of God, _______________ from all their infidelities, a _______________ which will include all the nations. Above all, the poor and _______________ of the Lord will bear this _________.   ***CCC 64***

3. Which prophet is mentioned in Daniel 14:33-39?

4. Describe Habakkuk's adventure in the Book of Daniel.   Daniel 14:33-39

5. Use a dictionary to define the term "oracle."

6. Against whom does Habakkuk complain?   Habakkuk 1:2

7. What is Habakkuk's complaint?   Habakkuk 1:2-4

8. Compare the following verses.

Habakkuk 1:5	
Acts 13:41	

9. Does God respond with a word of comfort or a warning of further trouble? Habakkuk 1:6-11

10. How is God depicted in the following passages?

Deuteronomy 32:4	
Deuteronomy 32:18	
2 Samuel 23:3	
Psalm 18:1-3	
Psalm 95:1	
Habakkuk 1:12	

11. What does Habakkuk say about God in Habakkuk 1:13-14?

12. Find an admonition and a comfort in Habakkuk 2:4.

13. Compare the following passages.

Habakkuk 2:4	
Romans 1:17	
Galatians 3:11	
Hebrews 10:38	

14. Describe "The Five Woes" identified in Habakkuk 2.

The Five Woes

Habakkuk 2:6-8		AGAINST ARROGANT GREED
Habakkuk 2:9-11		AGAINST PRESUMPTION
Habakkuk 2:12-14		AGAINST ___________
Habakkuk 2:15-17		AGAINST DEGRADING HUMAN DIGNITY
Habakkuk 2:18-20		AGAINST ___________

15. Use one word to describe Habakkuk 3:1-19.

16. What does Habakkuk ask of the Lord in Habakkuk 3:2?

17. List the positive attributes of God found in Habakkuk 3:3-4.

18. Describe the hope found in Habakkuk 3:13.

19. How does Habakkuk describe his relationship with the Lord?   Habakkuk 3:17-19

20. Write your own short prayer, hymn or canticle to the Lord in the space below.

JAMES 1-2
Real Faith Works

Memory Verse

"Let every man be quick to hear, slow to speak, slow to anger."

JAMES 1:19B

eet James. The author of the Letter of James introduces himself in the first verse: "James (Greek *Yakobos*), a servant of God and of the Lord Jesus Christ."

One of the most important people in the Old Testament is the patriarch Jacob, whose nickname was Israel, the father of the twelve sons who would become the twelve tribes of Israel. Jacob in Hebrew is *Yaaqob*, which is transliterated into Greek as *Yakobos*. The men in the New Testament known by the name James actually have the name Yakobos, or Jacob. For some reason, probably because of the popularity of this name among Christians, it has taken on many different forms in the European languages:
— Giacomo in Italian
— Jacques in French
— Jamis or James in English
— Seamus in Irish
— Hamish in Scottish
— Jaime or Iago (Santiago = Saint Iago = St. James) in Spanish

During the Middle Ages, many people went on pilgrimage to European shrines. The most popular, after the tombs of Sts. Peter and Paul in Rome, was the shrine of Santiago de Compostela in northwestern Spain. Even now, from seven different departure points in three countries, pilgrims begin their lengthy trek of 500 to 1000 miles through difficult country on foot, horseback or bicycle, in homage to St. James. In 1989, Pope John Paul II greeted 500,000 young *peregrinos* at Santiago for the Fourth World Youth Day.

In the Western European languages, the connection between the men bearing the name James in the New Testament and the Jacob of the Old Testament is obscured. In fact, they bear the same name, just as Joseph of the New Testament bears the same name as Joseph of the Old.

Jacob is one of the most common names among Jews, because Jacob was the father of all twelve tribes of Israel. Whereas the names Simon, Jude, Benjamin or Levi would be most common among members of those particular tribes, the name Jacob would be popular in all the tribes.

Hence it is not surprising that there are four New Testament figures who bear the name of James, which is actually the name Jacob:
— James son of Zebedee   — James son of Mary, wife of Clophas
— James son of Alphaeus   — James brother of the Lord.

Tradition has identified three of these listed here as one and the same person. Clophas and Alphaeus may be two forms of the same name, so that "James son of Alphaeus" and "James son of Mary wife of Clophas" may be two ways of designating the same person, probably the relative or kinsman (that is, the brother) of the Lord. Our certain list is reduced to two, then:
— James son of Zebedee, known as James the Greater
— James son of Alphaeus, known as James the Lesser

The author of the Letter of James does not tell us who his father was, but tradition ascribes the letter to James the Lesser, the first Bishop of Jerusalem. Certainly the author of this letter exercises great authority in the early Church, because he presumes to write a letter "to the twelve tribes in the dispersion." Only the pope in our day has the authority to write an official letter to the entire Catholic world. Any individual bishop who would attempt to do so would be overstepping his authority. James the Bishop of Jerusalem is the only New Testament James who would have the kind of position that would entitle him to write to the whole Christian world.

The term "the twelve tribes" seems to indicate a Jewish audience, and indeed at this early apostolic period most of the converts to Christianity were still Jewish. The God-fearing Gentiles who had converted were highly assimilated to Judaism for the most part at this early stage in church history. Hence, there is nothing anomalous or sectarian about James addressing his Christian audience by the term "the twelve tribes."

Why would the Bishop of Jerusalem write to everyone outside the Holy Land? For the first ten or twenty years of Church history, before the missionary journeys of St. Paul, evangelization took place mainly in Jerusalem itself. Jews and God-fearing Gentiles came to Jerusalem every year in large numbers for the feasts of Passover and Pentecost, and as we read in Acts it was in the context of the annual pilgrimage that the Holy Spirit descended upon James and the other apostles. They were inspired to preach the message of Jesus Risen to the crowds, five thousand of whom converted on the first Pentecost. Each year, as new crowds arrived, the apostles continued to preach the same message, and more were converted. In fact, those converted each year would go back to their home countries and spread the word among their friends, so that in succeeding years many would come with the specific intention of meeting the apostles and hearing their message. Over the course of two decades of catechesis, presided over by James in his function as Bishop of Jerusalem, many tens of thousands of Jews throughout the world had a chance to accept baptism and confirmation, and returned to their homes as Christians in good standing. Wherever St. Paul travels he encounters these scattered early Christians, products of the evangelization process supervised by St. James.

So, on reflection, why would the Bishop of Jerusalem write to everyone outside the Holy Land? It was precisely because he knew them, he had borne responsibility for their catechesis, and he knew that they needed his continued guidance. He wanted to ensure that they remained faithful to the teaching that they had received. Especially he wanted to answer certain questions that arose out of the teaching of St. Paul.

The term "servant of God and of the Lord Jesus Christ" deserves some comment. Jesus taught His disciples that those who exercised authority among them should serve the rest. The mother of James and John had sought positions of importance for her sons, but Jesus assured them that the only kind of privilege He had to bestow was that of service. The apostles argued

among themselves as to which was the greatest, but Jesus reminded them that they should seek to serve one another. James starts his letter by announcing not "I am James the Apostle," but "I am James the Servant." He had learned his lessons well. We are to see in the expression "servant of God" an ecclesiastical title of great distinction. Indeed, the Holy Father in Rome identifies himself as "the servant of the servants of God."

The Perfect Law of Freedom ~ Some translations render James' title at the top of the letter as "slave of God" [revised New American Bible]. This is too narrow. The word for servant is the same in Greek as the word for slave, but that does not mean the terms are interchangeable. All slaves were servants in ancient times, but not all servants were slaves. Many servants were freeborn and working for a salary. Jesus elsewhere in the New Testament says, "No longer do I call you servants, for the servant does not know what his master is doing; but I have called you friends" (John 15:15). St. Paul writes, "[Y]ou are no longer a slave, but a son" (Galatians 4:7).

Within the Letter of James, the theme of freedom appears in a very important context. In what is practically the most important summary of his entire message, James writes: "He who looks into the perfect law, the law of liberty, and perseveres, being no hearer that forgets but a doer that acts, he shall be blessed in his doing" (James 1:25). What is this "perfect law, the law of liberty?" James clarifies in the following chapter: "If you really fulfill the royal law, according to the scripture, 'You shall love your neighbor as yourself,' you do well" (James 2:8).

Here is a conjunction of the thought of James with that of John. John, as we saw a few chapters ago, disseminated the new commandment of loving one another after the pattern of Christ's love for us. At the heart of the theology of James is this same commandment, which he calls "the perfect law," "the law of liberty," and "the royal law." These two apostles understood love before they came to follow Christ, but they learned a new and higher form of love from Jesus; they could now love each other freed from competition and rivalries, freed by the example and teaching of their Lord. This set them free from the constraints of jealousy and rivalry, so that each could bear unique and great gifts of apostleship. John could exercise his ministry as an evangelist without looking over his shoulder at the authority wielded by James in Jerusalem, and vice versa. This is true freedom, the liberty to do what God wants each of us to do without the constraints of sinful thoughts.

Faith versus Works ~ St. Paul also speaks about "the freedom of the sons of God," which is the freedom *from* sin and the freedom *for* a true Christian way of life. However, the teaching of St. Paul about law versus gospel was apparently taken by some as indicating that none of us have to *do* anything. St. James corrects this misinterpretation of Pauline doctrine, when he writes: "Show me your faith apart from works, and I by my works will show you my faith" (James 2:18).

James had heard the Lord Himself say, "You will know them by their fruits" (Matthew 7:16), and had seen Jesus curse the fig tree that had borne no fruit (Mark 11:21). James knew that the Lord expected us to do something about our faith, because he had received Jesus' teaching, "Not everyone who says to me 'Lord, Lord' will enter the kingdom of heaven, but those who do the will of my Father who is in heaven" (Matthew 7:21). Jesus advocated no passivity before the grace of God, but encouraged His followers towards action by saying, "Blessed rather are those who hear the word of God and keep it" (Luke 11:28).

The teaching of the Letter of James follows close in its reasoning to the preaching of Jesus in the synoptic Gospels. Paul, on the other hand, never heard Jesus preach and so he uses a different kind of argumentation; he reacts so strongly against his background as a Pharisee that he almost goes too far, and James seeks to provide balance to Paul's writing. *Yes, faith in the heart is the source of all our responsiveness to God, but God never told anyone "Believe and do nothing about it."* Rather, if anything, belief is to be the first step in a very long journey towards God. The martyrs believed in the first instance, and gave their lives in the second. If they had died without faith, they would not be martyrs; but if they believed only and had not given their lives, they would not be martyrs either.

One school of Judaism saw the outward fulfillment of the law as the focus of religion. St. Paul reacts against that, with some vehemence. However, St. James provides a corrective balance. There has to be a concordance between the interior and the exterior life. No one can live a purely interior or an exclusively exterior faith. This is not a battle between James and Paul, but between Paul and the Pharisees, with James as referee. **Humble service to one another is for St. James, an exterior sign of interior faith.** That is why he says: "Religion that is pure and undefiled before God and the Father is this: to visit orphans and widows in their affliction, and to keep oneself unstained from the world" (James 1:27).

The life of St. James exemplifies his love for Christ and the Church. St. James the Less, Bishop of Jerusalem, was a prominent figure not only within the Christian community. Apparently his martyrdom in the 60's AD was a shock to many people, because the secular historian Josephus says:

> "(The procurator) Festus was now dead, and Albinus was but upon the road; so (Ananus the High Priest) assembled the Sanhedrin of judges, and brought before them the brother of Jesus who was called Christ, whose name was James, and some of his companions. And when he had formed an accusation against them as breakers of the law, he delivered them to be stoned."
>
> Josephus, *Antiquities of the Jews*, 20:9.1

The faith of St. James allowed him to make the supreme sacrifice to God, the offering of his very life in martyrdom for Christ and His Gospel. He knew that the grace of martyrdom would be given to him by the Giver of all good gifts, Who had even greater and more perfect gifts in store for him in heaven.

> "When we are baptized, we are enlightened. Being enlightened, we are adopted as sons. Adopted as sons, we are made perfect. Made perfect, we become immortal, sons all of the Most High. This work is variously called grace, illumination, perfection, and washing. It is a washing by which we are cleansed of sins; a gift of grace by which the punishments due our sins are remitted; an illumination by which we behold that holy light of salvation—that is, by which we see God clearly; and we call that perfection which leaves nothing lacking. Indeed, if a man knows God, what more does he need? . . . Because God is perfect, the gifts He bestows are perfect."
>
> St. Clement of Alexandria (150-211 AD), *The Instructor of Children*, 1.6.

1. How does the author of this letter identify himself in James 1:1?

2. What is the value of perseverance in trials and temptations?   James 1:2-4

Count/*consider* it all __________ when you meet various __________________ for you

know that the______________of your_______________produces ________________.

And let steadfastness/*perseverance* have its full effect that you may be ___________

and ____________, __________________in _____________________.   James 1:2-4

3. What should one do who lacks wisdom?   James 1:5-6

4. Does God tempt people?   James 1:13   *CCC 2846*

5. From where does temptation come? James 1:14-15

6. Where do "good gifts" originate? James 1:17-18

7. Be quick to _____________, slow to ___________, slow to ______________. James 1:19

8. What is expected along with hearing the word of God?   James 1:22-25

9. Write three characteristics of pure and undefiled religion.

James 1:26	
James 1:27	
James 1:27	

10. Who is called upon to demonstrate corporal works of mercy in this way? *CCC 2208*

11. James talks about the perfect law, the law of liberty. *CCC 1972*

The New Law is called _______________________________________

____

____

____

____

____

____

____

____

____

____. *CCC 1972*

12. Describe the admonition found in James 2:1-10.

13. "But if you show _____________________, you commit sin" (James 2:9).

14. List three practical ways that you can avoid the sin described above.

____

____

____

15. In your own words, describe the conflict in James 2:14-19.

16. Can you think of a situation depicted in literature or contemporary society in which someone's faith was demonstrated by their works?

17. Compare the following passages.

Matthew 25:34-39	
Galatians 5:6	*"...but faith _____________________ through love."*

18. How does the Bible respond to someone who claims that a man is saved by "Faith alone?"
    James 2:24

19. The Church's concern for the poor is modeled on Jesus' love for the poor.
    List below the spiritual and corporal works of mercy. *CCC 2447*

Spiritual Works of Mercy	*Corporal Works of Mercy*
(Pray for others in need)	

20. Circle one of the spiritual works of mercy and circle one of the corporal works of mercy.
    Do at least one work of mercy this week and write it down when you have done it.

JAMES 3-5
Wisdom from Above

Memory Verse

**"Whoever brings back a sinner from the error of his way
will save his soul from death and will cover a multitude of sins."**

JAMES 5:20

Saint James reveals his shepherd's heart for his flock as he offers sound, practical advice for the trials and temptations threatening his people. Like any good pastor, James offers concrete wisdom to the believers to equip them to ward off the attacks of their enemy, the devil. The same sage advice given centuries ago can benefit followers of Jesus Christ today, who ponder and take to heart these warnings and admonitions.

Much practical advice, starting with the dangers of the tongue—with the power to bless or to hurt, to build up or tear down—is recounted in James 3:2-12, 4:11-16 and 5:9. He warns about the strict judgment that teachers will face and cautions that not many should desire to become teachers (James 3:1). James compares and contrasts worldliness from godliness and advises his hearers to humble themselves to receive more of God's grace and resist the devil (James 4:6-10).

Rather than being ruled by passions and greed, the believer should seek wisdom from God (James 3:13-4:6). More practical wisdom comes in his encouragement to pray fervently and to bring the sick to the elders for anointing. Confession and intercession are encouraged by this shepherd for his flock, as well as encouragement to bring back the wayward from his sin (James 5:19-20).

Use of Parables ~ James uses a number of beautiful comparisons in the course of his writings. A comparison using the word "like" or "as" is called a simile, the large form of which is a parable.

James employs a number of smaller similes that remind us of the parables of Jesus:

— "[H]e who doubts is like a wave of the sea that is driven and tossed by the wind" (James 1:6).

— "[L]ike the flower of the grass he [the rich man] will pass away" (James 1:10).

— "[I]f any one is a hearer of the word and not a doer, he is like a man who observes his natural face in a mirror . . . and at once forgets what he was like" (James 1:23-24).

When the word "like" or "as" is not used in a comparison, it is called a metaphor. James uses the following metaphor: "The tongue is a fire" (James 3:6). A fire can warm the hearth and cook good food, but it can also destroy everything in its path when it gets out of control. So too, positive speech builds up the body of Christ, while rumors, grumbling, complaining and negative speech can burn individuals, wound spirits, destroy reputations, and divide the body of Christ.

James also uses some vivid images with the effect of a metaphor:

— "If we put bits into the mouths of horses that they may obey us, we guide their whole bodies" (James 3:3).

— "Look at the ships also; though they are so great and are driven by strong winds, they are guided by a very small rudder wherever the will of the pilot directs" (James 3:4).

— "How great a forest is set ablaze by a small fire!" (James 3:5).

— "Does a spring pour forth from the same opening fresh water and brackish?" (James 3:11).

— "Can a fig tree, my brethren, yield olives, or a grapevine figs?" (James 3:12).

— "[T]he farmer waits for the precious fruit of the earth, being patient over it until it receives the early and the late rain. You also must be patient" (James 5:7).

James makes a comparison between the rich man and the flower of the grass, similar to one of the images from the Sermon on the Mount, about the "lilies of the field." Some other comparisons that James makes are highly original and do not have any parallels elsewhere in the New Testament. James seems to have learned the parables from Jesus, but also goes on to use and develop original parables of his own. James shows himself to be both a good learner and a good teacher.

Specific Dangers of the Tongue ~ The distortion of the Christian message caused by some teachers in the diaspora provokes James to a highly poetic sermon against malicious speech. No one has ever analyzed the dangers of gossip better than James in this letter. What a wonderful comparison he makes when he points out that a forest fire begins with a single flame! Think before starting a rumor, which, like a forest fire, does so much damage and can hardly ever be stopped.

James' image of a spring, which cannot issue forth both fresh water and brackish water is highly original and very instructive. We bless God out of one side of our mouths and use His Holy Name as a curse word out of the other side of our mouths. Perhaps James foresaw all the blasphemous language that Christians would use down through the course of history. Moslems do not misuse the name of their prophet Mohammed; Buddhists never blaspheme the name of Buddha; and Jews take such care to avoid using the name of the Lord in vain that they never even pronounce the sacred name YHWH. Despite our belief in the divinity and perfect humanity of Jesus, Christians are the only major religious group that indulge in blasphemous speech on a habitual basis. Perhaps we should reread the Letter of James, who says, "My brethren, this ought not to be so" (James 3:10).

Thank God for the saints who have offered reparations to Almighty God for the misuse of the Name, at the mention of which "every knee should bow in heaven and on earth and under the earth" (Philippians 2:10). Think how the habitual blasphemy of many Christians impedes the work of evangelization and true witness, which we are supposed to offer to the entire world. Of course, the Christian tongue that misuses the Holy Name of Jesus is not likely to respect the good name and reputation of fellow human beings either. When St. James says that the tongue is "set on fire by hell," he gives an all-too-accurate description of the state of affairs.

James had received the Holy Spirit on Pentecost in the form of tongues of flame, and he had received the gift of tongues for the proclamation of the Christian message. The fires of Pentecost are more powerful than the fires of Hell, and the power of good speech is greater than that of foul speech. Every sin of commission is also a sin of omission. In speaking badly, we fail to say the good things that we should be saying. There is not time enough in one life for all the bad things we would like to do, nor all the good things too. Choose whether to live by malicious or spiritual language. The tongue can tear down or build up, destroy or edify. Apostleship requires giving good witness, and there is no time for bearing false witness against our neighbor in any apostolic life.

The Apostle as Prophet ~ St. James compares himself and the other apostles to the prophet Elijah: "Elijah was a man of like nature with ourselves" (James 5:17). He also counsels his listeners to live in a patient manner like the prophets before them: "As an example of suffering and patience, brethren, take the prophets who spoke in the name of the Lord. Behold, we call those happy who were steadfast. You have heard of the steadfastness of Job" (James 5:10-11).

The ministry of the apostles is a continuation of that of the prophets. The prophets heard God. Some of them saw Him, and went out to bear His word to others. The apostles knew Jesus, the Word of God, and then went out to the whole world to bear testimony to Him. In both cases, an experience of God is shared with others.

St. James clearly bases some of his comments, like the critique of riches, upon the prophetic tradition of Israel. As the letter progresses, it begins to sound more like Old Testament prophecy: "Come now, you rich, weep and howl for the miseries that are coming upon you" (James 5:1). Note the concern for social justice: "Behold, the wages of the laborers who mowed your fields, which you kept back by fraud, cry out" (James 5:4).

In both the Old and New Testaments, this critique of wealth is based not on the advocacy of class conflict, as in Marxism. The Old Testament prophet sees disaster coming for the people of Israel because the upper classes were more concerned with their own luxury than with the common good. He sees the futility of hoarding wealth when the city is about to be sacked. The New Testament apostle sees the second coming of Jesus Christ as near at hand, so the accumulation of worldly security is simply pointless. Obsession with wealth is a distraction from the service we need to render one another. The use of wealth for the common good and the advancement of the Kingdom of God provides a true service to God by those with the means to do so. We each must do what we can, and those with more have the opportunity and duty to do more accordingly.

James had a wealthy brother, a tax collector by the name of Levi, also known as Matthew. The New Testament never comes right out and says that they are brothers, but the Gospel of Mark calls each of them "Son of Alphaeus" (Mark 2:14 and 3:18) and that is not a common name. There is no Alphaeus anywhere in Old or New Testaments except the father of these two apostles. We have no way of knowing whether Alphaeus was rich or poor, but his son Matthew certainly acquired wealth. The richer brother Matthew and the poorer brother James heard Jesus say the words, "Blessed are the poor in spirit, for theirs is the kingdom of heaven." (Matthew 5:3) In response to these words, Matthew left much and James left less, but each left all to follow Jesus into the Kingdom.

From the prophetic tradition, James develops the teaching against partiality that is one of the earliest expressions of the fundamental equality of worth of all human beings: "My brethren, show no partiality as you hold the faith of our Lord Jesus Christ, the Lord of glory" (James 2:1). He notes the natural human inclination to show deference to those with wealth, but he teaches that our notice must go also to those whom society shuns. The elders of the church are to pray over the sick without regard to whether they are wealthy or poor (James 5:15). *James illustrates the Sacrament of the Anointing of the Sick, which is not reserved only for the dying, as once was the practice of the Church, but for any of the sick. He points out that this sacrament brings health of both body and soul, and that it brings both the potential for recovery and the surety of forgiveness.* Before such riches and power of grace, worldly wealth pales by comparison.

"God has given to priests powers greater than those given to our parents; and the differences between the powers of these two is as great as the difference between the future life and the present." Our parents begot us to temporal existence; priests beget us to the eternal. Parents are not able to ward off from their children the sting of death, nor prevent the attack of disease; yet priests often save the sick and perishing soul— sometimes by imposing a penance, sometimes by preventing the fall. Priests accomplish this not only by teaching and admonishing, but also by the help of prayer. Not only at the time of our regeneration (in baptism), but even afterward, they have the authority to forgive sins. 'Is there anyone among you sick? Let him call in the priests of the church, and let them pray over him, anointing him with oil in the name of the Lord. And the prayer of faith shall save the sick man, and the Lord shall raise him up, and if he have committed sins, he shall be forgiven.'"

St. John Chrysostom (344-407 AD), *The Priesthood*, 3.6.

The Letter of James ends abruptly, without the kind of farewell statement that is typical at the end of letters. The beginning had a proper salutation, but the end lacks any kind of valedictory. This might indicate that the end of the letter is missing. When scrolls were used it would have been quite easy for the bottom of the scroll to become detached. Another possibility is that what we really have here is not so much a letter as a sermon that has been sent around to other communities for the purpose of instruction and sharing its message. The opening salutation was necessary in order to identify the sender and the addressee, but from that point forwards the true literary form was that of a sermon, and not really an epistle. Remember that 1 John was more like a sermon, while 2 and 3 John had the form of true epistles. Some letters are really letters, and some are really sermons. The "Letter of James" reads like a really good sermon.

(Proverbs 13:3)

1. What does St. James warn about in the following passages?

James 3:2-12	
James 3:9, Psalm 62:4	
James 4:11-16	
James 5:9	

2. Write the encouragement for positive speech found in Proverbs 13:3.

3. Define these sins resulting from misuse of the tongue. *CCC 2477, 2479, 2481, 2482*

rash judgment	
detraction	
calumny	
boasting/bragging	
irony/negative speech	
lying	

4. List some advice on the proper use of the tongue from Sirach 23:7-15.

5. Provide some wisdom on the right use of the tongue from the passages below.

Psalm 19:14	
Psalm 34:1	
Psalm 51:15	
Psalm 141:3	
Proverbs 12:19	
Sirach 6:5	
Sirach 20:13	
James 5:12	

6. Describe the wisdom from above and its fruit.   James 3:13-18

7. What is wisdom and how can you get it?

Wisdom 1:1-6	
Psalm 111:10	
James 1:5	

8. How do conflicts and divisions originate? James 4:1-6

9. List the directives St. James gives in James 4:7-12.

10. In order to avoid presumption, what should you say?   James 4:13-17.

11. What similar advice do St. James and St. Peter offer in the following passages?

James 4:10	
1 Peter 5:6	
James 4:7-8	
1 Peter 5:8-9	

12. Compare the following warnings to the rich.

Luke 6:24	
James 5:1-6	
1 Timothy 6:17-19	

13. What does the Church encourage business owners to provide?

	CCC 2432
	CCC 2433
	CCC 2434

14. Tobit offers what advice to his son in Tobit 4:7-11 that the wealthy could heed?

15. Archangel Raphael provides more information on this topic in Tobit 12:8-10.

16. What virtues are necessary as we await the coming of the Lord?   James 5:7-11

17. What should a sick person do according to St. James?   James 5:13-18

18. What does the Catholic Church offer for the sick?   *CCC 1499*

____

____

____

____

____

____   *CCC 1499*

19. Where does the apostolic Church derive its rite for the anointing of the sick? *CCC 1510*

20. What is a believer's responsibility to a wayward brother, and what is the reward?

Ezekiel 33:8-9	
James 5:19-20	

21. Evaluate your speech this week. Have a friend or family member help you. Is your speech more positive or negative? Does your speech build up or tear down more? Check any of the following speech patterns that you observe.

_____ Praising	_____ Blessing	_____ Complimenting
_____ Encouraging	_____ Affirming	_____ Thanking
_____ Grumbling/Complaining	_____ Gossiping	_____ Swearing
_____ Putting Down	_____ Lying	

Rumor is a pipe
Blown by surmises, jealousies, conjectures,
And of so easy and so plain a stop
That the blunt monster with uncounted heads,
The still-discordant wavering multitude,
Can play upon it.

KING HENRY IV, WILLIAM SHAKESPEARE

A woman went to her priest, overwhelmed with guilt and remorse. She confessed that she had shared a little piece of negative information that she had learned about a friend in town. Now the rumor had spread throughout the community and the victim could hardly bear to be seen in public.

Whether the negative information was true or not, it reflected badly on the individual and the family of the person. The bad report grew with embellishments as different individuals speculated on the situation and added additional information. What could she do, now, to make amends? How could she repair the damage that had been done to this person?

Distraught, she sought the counsel of the priest. Father advised her to take a feather pillow to her upstairs window and tear the pillow open. Feathers flew across the countryside as if it were the blizzard of a winter snowstorm. The wind picked up each feather and tossed it about far and wide. When she had finished, the priest suggested that she go and collect all of the feathers.

"But, Father, that is impossible!" cried the woman in dismay.

"Yes, and it is just as impossible to retrieve the negative report that has been spread around our town and to restore your victim's privacy and good name."

Gossip holds a strange fascination for us

Monthly Social Activity

This month your small group will meet for coffee, tea, or a simple breakfast or lunch in someone's home.

Pray for this social event and for the host or hostess. Try, if at all possible, to attend. Offer hospitality for one of the socials to be held at your home.

A prophet is someone who speaks the word of the Lord. Can you think of a contemporary prophet who has fearlessly proclaimed the word of the Lord?

Now reflect on your own personal life.

> ~ Can you think of a person who has proclaimed the Word of the Lord to you?

> ~ Who taught you about Jesus?

> ~ Who has challenged you to follow the Lord more faithfully?

GALATIANS 1-2
Loyalty to the Gospel

Memory Verse

**"I have been crucified with Christ;
it is no longer I who live, but Christ who lives in me;
and the life I now live in the flesh I live by faith in the Son of God,
who loved me and gave himself for me."**

GALATIANS 2:20

ho were the Galatians? St. Paul actually says that he is writing to the "churches of Galatia." From these words we can understand that there were several cities included, each church being located in a different city within the same region, know as "Galatia," in present-day Turkey.

In the Book of Revelation, St. John receives messages for seven cities in western Asia Minor, and some of these cities were located in or near Galatia.

> "I was in the Spirit on the Lord's day, and I heard behind me a loud voice like a trumpet saying, 'Write what you see in a book and send it to the seven churches, to Ephesus and to Smyrna and to Pergamum and to Thyatira and to Sardis and to Philadelphia and to Laodicea.'"
> (Revelation 1:11)

Quite probably one or more of these cities were among those receiving the letter "to the Galatians." It is certain that the city of Pergamon (in Latin, Pergamum) was very closely bound up with the fate of the Galatian people.

The Galatians were Gauls, the same people who inhabited France, Spain and Britain in the last several centuries before Christ. Outstanding warriors, they offered their services as soldiers throughout the Mediterranean area. More than two centuries before Christ, King Attalus I of Pergamon invited Gallic mercenaries to come and fight for him, but they became so numerous that they ultimately became a threat to his throne. A terrible civil war ensued, resulting in a defeat for the Galatian forces.

King Attalus I took the name of "Soter" or "Savior" as a result, and he celebrated the victory by building one of the largest temples of the ancient world, the great Temple of Zeus on the highest hill, called "Acropergamon." A great bas-relief over six hundred feet long depicts the mythological battle between the gods and the giants, a heavenly corollary to the civil war that had taken place on earth. Along the top of the temple were magnificent bronzes depicting various Galatian warriors and civilians in grief and in death agonies. These masterpieces of Hellenistic art were so famous that sculptors later came from Rome and made marble copies, two of which still survive in Roman museums. The great "Dying Gaul" marble copy lies in the Capitoline Museum in Rome today; a sword pierces the warrior's side as he inclines on one arm with the lifeblood pouring out of him.

The poor Galatians were not only defeated in battle, but every time they came to the great city of Pergamon they would see themselves portrayed in agony on the highest point of the city. Their sufferings became propaganda for the regime, and art for the history books. For themselves, there could have been no artistic thrill in seeing these great works.

St. Paul found the Galatians more receptive than other people in the area to the Christian message of a Savior who had redeemed the world through His suffering. At the beginning of the letter, he proclaims, "Grace to you and peace from God the Father and our Lord Jesus Christ, who gave himself for our sins to deliver us from the present evil age" (Galatians 1:3-4). For the Galatians, downtrodden by history, the present age was certainly evil. Unlike the Athenians, who were scandalized by the idea of resurrection, as much as by that of the crucifixion (Acts 17:15-18:1), the Galatians could identify with the sufferings of Christ and be thrilled by the teaching of the resurrection on the other side of suffering.

Stressing this identification between our sufferings and those of Christ, St. Paul writes, "I have been crucified with Christ" (Galatians 2:20). At the end of the letter he summarizes, "But far be it from me to glory except in the cross of our Lord Jesus Christ, by which the world has been crucified to me, and I to the world" (Galatians 6:14). St. Paul even adds this detail, which seems to indicate that he bore the stigmata ten centuries before St. Francis of Assisi: "I bear on my body the marks of Jesus" (Galatians 6:17).

The Galatians had spent their whole lives with their psyches branded by the bronzes of the dying Gauls in Pergamon. Their spirits were wounded when they beheld the sword mark in the side of their defeated kinsman. Ironically, this Hellenistic propaganda prepared them to understand the salvific power of the death of Jesus. It is no surprise, then, that northwestern Asia Minor, the area of Galatia, was the first part of the Roman Empire to embrace Christianity in substantial numbers. A sizeable percentage of the population was baptized before the end of the apostolic period.

The Crucifix shows the corpus, or the body of Christ, at the moment of death. The origins of the Crucifix as art lies in the dying Galatians of Pergamon. Even the wounded side of the Dying Gaul prefigures the wounded side of Christ. A people that had known and understood suffering could and did take up the Cross of Christ, and many of them were willing to die for the faith.

What does St. Paul say about himself? The first two chapters of the Letter to the Galatians present a capsule autobiography from St. Paul himself. The account is authenticated by the fact that he refers to St. Peter not by the Greek form of his name, but by the Aramaic form "Cephas" (Galatians 1:18, 2:9, 11). Jesus always spoke Aramaic rather than Greek to Simon Peter; so when He gave him the nickname, "The Rock," it was in the Aramaic, "Cephas." The apostles spoke Aramaic among themselves; so they all called Simon Peter, "Cephas." Only after he set out to evangelize the Greeks of Antioch did the head of the apostles come to be known by the Greek translation, "Petros."

The little autobiography in Galatians matches up pretty well with St. Luke's more extensive biographical treatment of Paul in the Acts of the Apostles. Of course, St. Luke offers many more details from a slightly different point of view. St. Luke had been St. Paul's traveling companion and drew his materials directly from the source and his personal observation. In Galatians, St. Paul gives a time line for his life, and these numbers are probably not symbolic

"biblical numbers" but literal arithmetic: "Then after three years I went up to Jerusalem to meet Cephas, and remained with him fifteen days" (Galatians 1:18). "Then after fourteen years I went up again to Jerusalem with Barnabas" (Galatians 2:1).

Doing the math, we learn that seventeen years had transpired (three plus fourteen) between St. Paul's conversion and the beginning of his public ministry. Now, Jewish rabbis did not begin to function until they reached the age of 30, the same age at which Romans of senatorial rank could take their seat in the chambers and begin to hold administrative office. Hence, Jesus began His public ministry at age thirty, and St. John the Baptist, who was born exactly six months before Jesus, began his public ministry precisely six months before Jesus, too.

If St. Paul began his ministry to the nations at age 30, then counting back 17 years he would have been only 13 years old at the time of his conversion! Impossible? From the time of his bar-mitzvah at age 12, he could find a teacher and function as an adult disciple. St. John was probably in his early teens when he accepted the call of Jesus and followed Him. Paul attached himself to Gamaliel, one of the great teachers in Israel in the time of Jesus, and one of the early founders of rabbinic Judaism. As a "young man," Saul holds the coats of those stoning St. Stephen (Acts 7:59). He was thus far too young to begin his public ministry at the time of his conversion, and had to spend nearly two decades in further study and preparation. Most of that time St. Paul spent in his hometown of Tarsus, working at a manual trade (tent-making) as was customary to rabbis in training.

<table>
<tr><td>

If Jesus was teaching the doctors in the temple at age 12, then Saul could have been similarly precocious at age 13. Can you visualize Paul filled with all the fanaticism that the young can show when they are enlisted in a "cause?" He says of himself, "I advanced in Judaism beyond many of my own age" (Galatians 1:14). Perhaps the elders sent him to Damascus, not so much to persecute the Christians as to get rid of him. In any event, giving an occasional reading in the synagogue or sermon in the Temple is one thing, having a full-blown public ministry is another. He had to be at least thirty years old for the latter.

</td></tr>
</table>

Contrast the statements St. Paul makes about his apostleship with those in the First Letter of St. John. Where St. John stresses that apostles were those who had known and heard and touched the Word made Flesh while He was among us (1 John 1:1-2), St. Paul seems to take pride in the fact that his experience of the Lord was purely spiritual. St. Paul did not become an apostle the same way that St. John or the other Twelve had, but the same Lord called them both and for the same purpose. Since they were about the same age, and even wrote to some of the same churches, they must have operated in the same area and possibly even at the same time. St. Paul's ministry ended in martyrdom some thirty years before the death of St. John, the only apostle not called to give his life for Christ.

In these very early years when St. Paul was writing, the original apostles were still living and had not yet ordained many successors such as St. Matthias (Acts 1:26). St. Paul sounds somewhat insecure and needing to assert his authentic apostleship over against the original apostles, whom he calls those "reputed to be pillars" (Galatians 2:9).

Note that St. Paul mentions both Cephas and James twice. The first time he mentions them in that order (Galatians 1:18-19), but the second time he reverses the order, listing "James and Cephas and John" (Galatians 2:9). The listing of James before John is normative in the New Testament, for James was the elder brother and should be listed first. Luke calls them "James and John, sons of Zebedee" when they are called (Luke 5:10), but later deviates from custom in mentioning "Peter and John and James" (Luke 9:28). When St. Paul inserts Cephas between the two brothers, he seems to demote Cephas to a lower position than that of James. Actually, St. James wielded great authority in the early Church as the Bishop of Jerusalem, and perhaps inside the city itself, Cephas deferred to him. Moreover, James was apparently a very common name among Jews at that time, so it becomes very difficult to identify which James is which in each biblical reference.

Paul probably made a number of trips to Jerusalem, of which only several are mentioned in the Bible. The trips mentioned by Luke may or may not correspond to the ones mentioned in Galatians. According to Luke, Barnabas went up to get Saul and rescue him from obscurity (Acts 11:25). After one year in Antioch (Acts 11:26), Barnabas and Saul travel to Jerusalem (Acts 11:30). Only after that trip does St. Luke list Saul among the prophets and teachers in Antioch (Acts 13:1). So it is doubtful to say that the trip was "at the beginning of his ministry" in a rough sense.

St. Paul stresses his confrontation with the head of the apostles in Antioch—note that it did not take place in Jerusalem. St. Peter was now on new ground. The issue was an important one: Should Christians of Jewish origin eat at table with Christians of Gentile origin? Table fellowship was very important in the Greek world. Admission to communion in the Catholic Church reflects this ancient custom and presupposes a common theology, understanding and acceptance of the truth of the Real Presence of Christ in the Eucharist. In this case, however, St. Paul criticizes the actions of St. Peter for failing to have the courage of his convictions. St. Peter had begun to eat with Gentile Christians, and then ceased doing so after receiving pressure from Jerusalem. St. Paul wanted to ensure that the first pope remained true to the idea of one church, not two. If the two sets of Christians couldn't eat together then, how many churches would there eventually have been?

> "That rule is to be held which confesses that the Son is in the Father, and the Father is in the Son; which acknowledges the arrangement of the Godhead by observing that there is one substance in two Persons. Therefore the Father is God, and the Son is God, because God the Son is in God the Father. And if this be a scandal to anyone, let him hear from us that the Spirit is from God: for He that has in the Son a Second Person has also a Third in the Holy Spirit. . . . The Lord says 'I shall ask of My Father and He will give you another Advocate' (John 14:16).
>
> . . . All however, are one God. The Three are One. This we believe, this we hold, because this we have received from the Prophets, this do the Gospels tell us, this the Apostles handed down, this the martyrs confessed by their suffering. In this we adhere to the faith even with our faculties of mind—against which even if an angel of heaven pronounce, let him be anathema (Galatians 1:8)."
>
> St. Foebad of Agen, (+ 392 AD), *Against the Arians*, 22.

1. Why did God send Jesus to earth? Galatians 1:1-5

2. What is the true center and essence of the apostolic faith? *CCC 442*

3. What does Paul suggest should happen to someone who preaches a false gospel?
    Galatians 1:6-10

4. List some contemporary examples of false gospels or false prophets.

5. Explain what St. Paul means when he speaks of "the church of God" in Galatians 1:13?

In Christian usage the word "church"____

____

____

____

____

____

____

____.   *CCC 752*

6. How did Paul receive the gospel? Galatians 1:11-24

7. How do we get faith?   Galatians 1:15, *CCC 153*

Faith is a ___________________

When St. Peter confessed that ___________________________________

____

____

____

____

____

____

____

____

____

____. *CCC 153*

8. Describe Saul's conversion from the following passages.

<u>Acts 9:1-22</u>	<u>Acts 22:4-16</u>	<u>Acts 26:12-18</u>

9. How is Paul established as an apostle? *CCC 659*

10. What goal does Paul express in Galatians 2:5?

11. To which different tasks did God called Peter and Paul? Galatians 2:7-9

12. God continues to call people to different tasks or ministries. Has there been a time when you may have thought that your calling was "the only calling" or the "best ministry in the church?"

13. How does Paul describe the reputations of Peter, James and John in Galatians 2:9?

14. Describe the problem in Galatians 2:11-14.

15. How are you justified before God? Galatians 2:15-18, Romans 3:24

Galatians 2:15-18	
Romans 3:24	

16. Does God love you?   John 3:16, Isaiah 43:1, Isaiah 49:15, *CCC 616*

John 3:16	
Isaiah 43:1	
Isaiah 49:15	
CCC 616	

17. What is a sign of God's love for you? Galatians 2:20, *CCC 478*

Jesus knew and loved us __________ and __________ during his life, his agony, and his Passion and gave himself up for _________ _________ of us: "The Son of God...loved _______ and gave himself for ______." He has loved ___________ ____________ with a ____________ ____________. For this reason, the______________ _____________ of _______________, pierced by our sins and for our salvation, "is quite rightly considered the ______________ __________ and symbol of that ... love with which the divine __________________ continually ______________ the eternal Father and __________ human beings" ________________ exception.   *CCC 478*

18. What means has God provided to remain present with you in a sacrament of love? *CCC 1380*

19. How can you welcome the Son of God who loves you into your midst? *CCC 2666*

20. According to Paul's example, how should one live? Galatians 2:20

GALATIONS 3-4
Adoption into Christ

Memory Verse

**"But when the time had fully come,
God sent forth his Son, born of woman, born under the law,
to redeem those who were under the law,
so that we might receive adoption as sons."**

GALATIANS 4:4-5

Foolish Galatians! Insulting one's audience is something that no speaker should ever, ever do. Here Paul seems to go too far. Clearly, he is pushing the envelope. Yet he gets away with it—who saved this letter so that it could become part of the New Testament? Nobody other than the Galatians, the very ones whom he seems to be insulting!

Paul can get away with this harsh language for two reasons:

(a) Clearly there is a lot of love between Paul and the Galatians, and they are already accustomed to his brusque style. He has probably already insulted them once or twice before, and perhaps in even harsher terms than these. Remember that in the last chapter, Paul said that Peter "stood condemned." The Galatians might have thought they got off easily only being called foolish.

(b) The terminology is not as insulting as it sounds. The Galatians have already become familiar with Paul's way of thinking. They know that, according to Paul, superior intelligence of a worldly sort is no advantage in the Kingdom of God. When Paul calls them foolish, it is not exactly a back-handed compliment. Reflect on Paul's words to the Corinthians.

> "For the word of the cross is folly to those who are perishing, but to us who are being saved it is the power of God. For it is written, 'I will destroy the wisdom of the wise, and the cleverness of the clever I will thwart.' Where is the wise man? Where is the scribe? Where is the debater of this age? Has not God made foolish the wisdom of the world?" (1 Corinthians 1:18-20).

The Galatians may be a little slow to understand Paul's arguments, but clearly their hearts are in the right place. Paul does not regard their lack of mental acumen as any kind of impediment to their eventual progress in the Spirit. In fact, they have some unlearning to do before they can begin to learn.

The problem here is their gullibility. Paul comes and tells them the message, then someone else comes and gives them another. Different itinerant preachers present their messages, and the Galatians become confused. Perhaps, as children do, they play one father figure off against another. Paul makes this game unpleasant for them, so that they won't want to keep it up.

Abraham's Faith ~ Now the tone of the letter changes. In the first two chapters, Paul was laying his own life's story before the Galatians, to bear witness to his faith before them. Now Paul enters into a technical, theological treatise. He has just insulted the Galatians' intelligence, but now he honors them by giving them one of the finest and clearest expositions of his doctrine to be found anywhere in his letters. The heart of the Letter to the Galatians is his explanation of the relationship between law and faith. A longer version of this treatise can be found in the Letter to the Romans. Many parallel passages can also be found between Galatians 3 and Romans 4.

What then shall we say about Abraham, our forefather according to the flesh? For if Abraham was justified by works, he has something to boast about, but not before God. For what does the scripture say? "Abraham believed God, and it was reckoned to him as righteousness" (Romans 4:1-3).	Does he who supplies the Spirit to you and works miracles among you do so by works of the law, or by hearing with faith? Thus Abraham "believed God and it was reckoned to him as righteousness." So you see that it is men of faith who are the sons of Abraham (Galatians 3:5-7).

As you can see, Paul quotes Genesis 15:6 in both of these letters, and he finds the figure of Abraham a crucial determining factor in his thinking about faith. Paul wants to extend the Kingdom of God to people of every nation. This project is the fulfillment of God's promise to Abraham to become the father of many nations.

Other apostles were telling Gentile people that they had to accept the Mosaic law in order to enter the Kingdom of God. However, the Law of Moses in its fulness was never intended to be for every nation on the face of the earth, but only for one nation on the face of the earth—the Jewish nation. Judaism has never been a proselytizing religion. Jews have accepted converts, but they have never gone out of their way to make them. They have accepted the Mosaic law for themselves, and have never seen anyone else as bound by it or needing it.

How, then, can non-Jews be saved? This widely discussed question generated several opinions within Judaism. Most rabbis believed that Gentiles had to accept only the ethical teachings of the law, and they could then be saved. Eventually the Rabbis came up with the solution that Gentiles had to avoid three sins—idolatry, murder and adultery (in other words to obey Commandments One, Five and Six). This accords perfectly with the judgment of the apostles assembled at the Council of Jerusalem: "For it has seemed good to the Holy Spirit and to us to lay upon you no greater burden than these necessary things: that you abstain from what has been sacrificed to idols and from blood and from what is strangled and from unchastity. If you keep yourselves from these, you will do well" (Acts 15:28-29).

Paul sees the Covenant of Moses as a small umbrella, but the Covenant of Abraham as a big tent. His mission is not to attack and destroy the Covenant of Moses. He states clearly in Romans, "Do we then overthrow the law by this faith? By no means!" (Romans 3:31).

Paul points out very clearly and correctly that circumcision was not part of Abraham's original covenant with God. Abraham received the promise first, and only several decades later was the practice of circumcision imposed. All Abraham had to do at first was to believe

in the promise. God's original covenant was a treaty with no obligations on Abraham's part, but only on God's. This pristine covenant was pure gift, and not an exchange of obligations as in the usual matter of treaties.

Paul links Abraham directly with Christ, because Christ is Abraham's ultimate heir, the ultimate fulfillment of God's promise to Abraham that he would have a descendant. What a descendant! Of all Abraham's many descendants, starting with Ishmael, going on to Isaac, and through them to many others, Christ is the one descendant of whom Abraham can be most proud.

Adoption in Christ ~ By faith in Christ we achieve adoption into Christ. Paul calls this "adoption as sons" (Galatians 4:5). The actual Greek term here is "Sonship." Now the meat grinder of modern feminism has made mincemeat of Paul's terminology here. Paul is not saying anything about masculinity or femininity here. Remember, he has just said "There is neither Jew nor Greek, there is neither slave nor free, there is neither male nor female; for you are all one in Christ Jesus" (Galatians 3:28). Nonetheless, he goes on to use the term "Sonship" to describe our assumed status before the Father. It just will not work to play around with Paul's terminology and turn "Sonship" into "childhood" or "dependency" or the like. The richness of the meaning is distorted. The fourth chapter of Galatians contains one of the most important statements in all of the inspired Scripture:

> But when the time had fully come, God sent forth his Son, born of woman, born under the law, to redeem those who were under the law, so that we might receive adoption as sons. And because you are sons, God has sent the Spirit of his Son into our hearts, crying "Abba! Father!" So through God you are no longer a slave but a son, and if a son then an heir.
>
> (Galatians 4:4-7)

Count the number of times that the word "son" appears in those verses. The number is six. There is nothing symbolic about this number, it is just a highly frequent occurrence in three short verses. Twice the word refers to Christ, and so in these cases it is capitalized. The other four times, the word refers to the reader and is left in lower case. See how Paul is using the same word to refer to you and to Christ. He is making an identification; he is saying that through adoption into the Sonship of Christ you are acquiring the same relationship to the Father that Christ has.

Whenever you go into a bookstore and see a "new translation" of the Bible, open it to these verses and see what the translators have done with it. Some of the people in your small group may have some of these translations, which will make a fruitful comparison. You may be amazed by some of them. Usually we don't compare different translations in this series, but on this occasion, because of the importance of this passage, consider the damage done to Paul's good work.

> *"But when the fullness of time had come, God sent God's Child, born of woman, born under the law, in order to redeem those who were under the law, so that we might receive adoption as children. And because you are children, God has sent the Spirit of God's Child into our hearts, crying, "Abba! Father-Mother!" So you are no longer enslaved but rather you are a child, and if a child then also an heir, through God"*
>
> *(Galatians 4:4-7, New Testament and Psalms An Inclusive Version, Oxford, 1995).*

This demonstrates perhaps the worst translation that has appeared in print, but many recent versions show the same bad tendencies. The translators may be well-intentioned. They want to ensure that women do not feel excluded from the text. Changing the essential terminology, however, excludes all readers, men and women, from understanding what Paul really said. The translation is no longer transparent, but clouded. When the Pauline language is altered, the Pauline logic collapses. Instead of including everyone, the translator has managed to exclude everyone from adoption into Christ.

Abba Father ~ You may remember that earlier in Galatians, Paul referred to Peter not once but twice by the Aramaic form of his name, Cephas. Now, Paul uses another important Aramaic word, *Abba*, which means "The Father." (It does not mean "Father-Mother." That would be *Abba-Umma* in Aramaic.)

The word for Father in both Aramaic and Hebrew is *Ab*. Hebrew speakers attach the definite article as a prefix to the noun, so "The Father" in Hebrew become *Ha-Ab*. Aramaic speakers put the definite article as a suffix attached to the end of the noun, so "The Father" in Aramaic becomes *Ab-Ah* or *Abba*.

Certainly Jesus, as a native Aramaic speaker, used the term *Abba* to refer to His Father continually throughout His public ministry. He would say things like "Abba and I are one," or "No one can come to Abba except through me." The four evangelists managed to translate Jesus' terminology into Greek, except in one passage where St. Mark allows the original terminology to slip through: "Abba, Father, all things are possible to thee; remove this cup from me, yet not what I will but what thou wilt" (Mark 14:36). Note the powerful force to this verse, because the original word of Jesus breaks through the translation to reveal His Heart of love for His Father.

There are only three times in the whole New Testament where the Aramaic original *Abba* appears in the existing text—there in Mark, here in Galatians, and in a passage of Romans that is quite similar to this one in Galatians.

<blockquote>
For all who are led by the Spirit of God are sons of God. For you did not receive the spirit of slavery to fall back into fear, but you have received the spirit on sonship. When we cry "Abba! Father!" it is the Spirit himself bearing witness with our spirit.

(Romans 8:14-16)
</blockquote>

By using this word here in Galatians and there in Romans, Paul shows how close he is to the language of Jesus. Paul never met Jesus personally before His death and resurrection, but they spoke the same tongue. Paul called his own father "Abba," and Jesus called St. Joseph "Abba." Jesus called His heavenly Father "Abba" and taught His disciples to pray:

"Our Abba who art in heaven, hallowed be Thy name."

1. How was Jesus portrayed to the Galatians? Galatians 3:1

2. Can the human face of Jesus be portrayed? Are paintings of Jesus Christ and depictions of His body (corpus) on a crucifix acceptable or a sin of idolatry? Since when? *CCC 476*

3. How did the Galatians begin their spiritual journey? Galatians 3:1-3

4. What can justify a person before God? Galatians 3:4-9

5. Explain Christ's relationship with the law. Galatians 3:10-14

6. Look to the Catechism for further discussion of Jesus and the Law.

Jesus, Israel's Messiah ____

____

____

____

____

____

_______________________ This is why every year on the Day of Atonement the children of Israel ask God's forgiveness for the transgressions of the Law.   *CCC 578*

7. Who is cursed by the Law? Galatians 3:10-20

> The perfect fulfillment of the law ______________________________
> ____
> ____
> ____
> ____
> ____
> ____
> ____
> ____. ***CCC 580***

8. Why did God give the Law?

Galatians 3:21-24	
CCC 708	

9. Is the Law good or bad? What good does it do? ***CCC 1963***

10. How can you "put on Christ?" Galatians 3:27 ***CCC 1227***

11. Who is entitled to say "Our Father?" ***CCC 1243***

12. Explain the difference between an heir and a slave. Galatians 4:1-9

13. Explain the power prompting you to say "Abba! Father!" Galatians 4:6-7

14. How did Jesus pray in the following situations.

Matthew 6:9-15	
Mark 14:36	
Luke 11:2-4	

15. What sacrament first brings us in touch with Christ, and by whose power? *CCC 683*

16. Identify some titles of the Holy Spirit.

Galatians 3:4	
Galatians 4:6	
Romans 8:9	
2 Corinthians 3:17	
1 Peter 4:14	

17. What did Paul do for the Galatians? Galatians 4:12-20

18. Compare the following verses.

Isaiah 54:1-2	
Galatians 4:27	

19. Explain the allegory Paul makes about the two covenants from these passages.

Genesis 21:9-12	
Galatians 4:21-31	

20. Who is our mother?

Galatians 4:26	
CCC 757	
CCC 723	

GALATIANS 5-6
The Fruit of the Spirit

Memory Verse

**"But the fruit of the Spirit is love, joy, peace, patience,
kindness, goodness, faithfulness, gentleness, self-control:
against such there is no law."**

GALATIANS 5:22-23

Paul seems concerned in chapter 5 of Galatians that his readers not get the impression that his anti-legalistic rhetoric be an invitation to libertarianism. The Gospel places parameters of love on our behavior. As he says, "For you were called to freedom, brethren; only do not use your freedom as an opportunity for the flesh, but through love be servants of one another" (Galatians 5:13).

Although we are not to live by law, Paul gives a litany of negative behaviors that we should avoid because of the Gospel: "Now the works of the flesh are plain: immorality, impurity, licentiousness, idolatry, sorcery, enmity, strife, jealousy, anger, selfishness, dissension, party spirit, envy, drunkenness, carousing, and the like" (Galatians 5:19-20). We have not been so liberated from the Mosaic law that we can become idolaters of the flesh.

Then, immediately, however, Paul provides us with a description of the positive behaviors that we should expect of Christians. "But the fruit of the Spirit is love, joy, peace, patience, kindness goodness, faithfulness, gentleness, self-control; against such there is no law" (Galatians 5:22-23). St. Jerome translated the whole Bible into the language of the people and his translation became normative for the Roman Catholic Church for 1600 years. Consider what this patron saint of biblical scholars, St. Jerome, has to say about this passage in Galatians.

"The fruit of the Spirit, however, is love, joy, peace, patience, kindness, goodness, faith, modesty, continence, against which there is no law (Galatians 5:22-23). And what other one of the fruits of the Spirit ought to be given the primary place, if not love, without which the other virtues are not rightly virtues at all, and from which all other good things come.

"While we have time, therefore, let us do good to all, especially, however, to those of the household of the faith (Galatians 6:10). The time for sowing, as we have said, is the present time, and in the life we now lead. In this life we can sow what we will; but when this life is over, the time for works is at an end. Whence the Savior says: "Work while it is yet day; the night will come when none shall be able to work' (John 9:4)."

St. Jerome (347-420 AD), *Commentary on the Epistle to the Galatians,* 3.5.

It should be clear that Paul, in dispensing the Gentiles from Mosaic law, had no intention of condemning good deeds as such. He disparages "the works of the Law" (meaning circumcision and kosher diet) and "the works of the flesh" (fornication and anger), but he never disparages "good deeds." Paul agrees, then, that we are not saved by a strictly interior experience of grace. "If we live by the Spirit, let us also walk by the Spirit" (Galatians 5:25). We draw very close to the theology of St. James at this point. The teachings of the two apostles reach a point of convergence here. Freedom is their common theme—freedom *for* and not just freedom *from*.

For you were called to freedom, brethren; only do not use your freedom as an opportunity for the flesh, but through love be servants of one another. For the whole law is fulfilled in one word, "You shall love you neighbor as yourself" (Galatians 5:13-14).	But he who looks into the perfect law, the law of liberty, and perseveres, being no hearer that forgets but a doer that acts, he shall be blessed in his doing. . . . If you really fulfil the royal law, according to the scripture, "You shall love your neighbor as yourself," you do well (James 1:25, 2:8).

The Nature of Paul's Bodily Ailment ~ Paul suggests that because of a bodily ailment, he made the acquaintance of the Galatians. "You know that it was because of a bodily ailment that I preached the gospel to you at first; and though my condition was a trial to you, you did not scorn or despise me, but received me as an angel of God, as Christ Jesus" (Galatians 4:13-14).

We have no proof of what Paul's specific medical condition was, but there are hints offered along the way. One possibility suggests itself right in the very next verse: "For I bear you witness that, if possible, you would have plucked out your eyes and given them to me" (Galatians 4:15). Now, what good would the Galatians' eyes have been to Paul, unless his own eyes were weakened, diseased or deficient in some way?

Recall that after his encounter with the Risen Lord Jesus on the road to Damascus, Paul was blinded for three days. When Ananias prayed over him, something like scales fell from his eyes, and he could see (Acts 9:8-18). That sounds something like cataracts, doesn't it?

On another occasion, at the climax of the powerful and beloved "Love is patient" chapter of First Corinthians, Paul uses one of his most poetic images: "For now we see in a mirror dimly" (1 Corinthians 13:12). An older, more familiar translation went "through a glass, darkly." Perhaps the older translation captured the image better. There is nothing necessarily dim about a mirror, unless it is a very old and opaque one, for a mirror will reflect the sun's rays enough to start a fire. On the other hand, glasswork in Paul's day was a very recent technological breakthrough, and Roman glass was not yet clear and transparent as modern glass is. Ancient glass tended to be opaque, and looking at the world through glass would have produced a definite darkening. What we may have here is not just a poetic image but a description of what the world looked like to a person whose sight was impaired, in the days before corrective lenses or eye surgery.

Another indication of eye trouble comes during the valedictory at the end of this letter, when Paul says, "See with what large letters I am writing to you with my own hand"(Galatians 6:11). We know from other letters that Paul would dictate his letter to a secretary, and then he would write out the last few sentences himself.

At the end of Romans, Paul's secretary throws in a little greeting of his own. "I, Tertius, the writer of this letter, greet you in the Lord." Interestingly, the secretary of the letter to the Romans has a Latin name. Tertius means "third" and was commonly borne by the third son in a Roman family (as the name Quintus was borne by the fifth, Sextus by the sixth).

Three Pauline letters contain the concluding statement, "I, Paul, write this greeting with my own hand" (1 Corinthians 16:21, Colossians 4:18, 2 Thessalonians 3:17). It is clear that the bodies of those letters were written by someone else, perhaps the person associated with Paul in the opening greeting: Sosthenes at the beginning of First Corinthians, Timothy at the beginning of Second Corinthians and Colossians.

His secretary for First Corinthians was probably Sosthenes, who is mentioned in the opening verse of the letter: "Paul, called by the will of God to be an apostle of Christ Jesus, and our brother Sosthenes" (1 Corinthians 1:1). Timothy may have been the scribe for Second Corinthians and Colossians, which both begin: "Paul, an apostle of Christ Jesus by the will of God, and Timothy our brother" (2 Corinthians 1:1 and Colossians 1:1). The two letters to the Thessalonians are addressed from Silvanus and Timothy along with Paul.

The upshot of all this is the fact that Paul needed someone else to write his correspondence for him. He certainly was not illiterate, for he wrote the valedictories on several of the letters personally. The elephant in the living room is that Paul may have had trouble with his vision. At the end of Galatians, he calls attention to his handwriting: "See with what large letters I am writing to you with my own hand" (Galatians 6:11). The terminology may refer not just to the size of the handwriting, but also to the use of capital letters rather than small case letters. That is the way young children write, or foreigners, or people who are visually impaired. Taken together with the other indications of eye problems that Paul had even from his younger years, this adds a strong link to our chain of reasoning.

We may or may not be correct in concluding that the nature of Paul's ailment was ocular. Nevertheless, the fact is that he himself says that he met the Galatians initially because of that ailment. Why would that be?

Well, it so happens that the greatest medical facility in the Roman world existed in Pergamon, the same city that is associated historically with Galatians, as mentioned earlier in our commentary. There was a great shrine to Asklepios, the Greek god of healing, in Pergamon. There, at the so-called Asklepion, priests and medics attended the sick. In addition to the prayers and sacrifices for healing that were offered there, a body of anecdotal knowledge accumulated from the observation of many patients. At Pergamon, in the second century AD, there lived one of the founders of the science of medicine, the anatomist, physiologist and physician, Galen. Galen, a genius and pioneer, did not exist in a vacuum. His advances were made possible by the clinical environment at the Asklepion.

People from all over the Roman Empire and even beyond went to Pergamon for medical help. If Paul had done so, whether for his eyes or whatever his health problem may have been, he would have lodged with local Christians, the Galatians. Hence, it would be literally true that "it was because of a bodily ailment that I preached the gospel to you at first" (Galatians 4:13).

A troubling verse of this letter makes better sense in this light. Speaking of circumcision, Paul says, "I wish those who unsettle you would mutilate themselves!" (Galatians 5:12). Literally what he says is, "I wish the knife would slip." This shocking statement has the ring of professional jargon and may reflect some colloquialism addressed largely to members of the medical community. The Galatians lived near a shrine that was one of the principal centers of therapeutic surgery in the whole world at that time. This sort of speech may have been common in that environment, explaining Paul's unusual choice of words.

Pauline scholars today believe that the members of the pro-circumcision party were not Judaeo-Christians but Gentile converts who wanted, through circumcision, to disguise themselves as Jews so they would not be subject to persecution as Christians. Judaism was an approved religion of the Roman Empire, but Christianity was not. Paul's opponents were not Jews but Judaizers, who shrouded themselves in the appearance of Judaism. Several of Paul's remarks seem to confirm this opinion. "For even those who receive circumcision do not themselves keep the law" (Galatians 6:13).

Finally, although alluding to them, Paul does not display his scars for us to see, or describe his medical symptoms. Had he done so, we would know more certainly what modern medicine would say about his condition. More important to him than his own words were those of Christ. "But far be it from me to glory except in the cross of our Lord Jesus Christ, by which the world has been crucified to me, and I to the world" (Galatians 6:14).

St. Paul describes in a particularly eloquent way the tension and struggle that trouble the human heart. There already exists in man, as a being made up of body and spirit, a certain tension, a certain struggle of tendencies between the "spirit" and the "flesh." But this struggle in fact belongs to the heritage of sin, is a consequence of sin and at the same time a confirmation of it. This is part of everyday experience. As the Apostle writes: "Now the works of the flesh are plain: fornication, impurity, licentiousness . . . drunkenness, carousing and the like." These are the sins that could be called "carnal." But he also adds others: "enmity, strife, jealousy, anger, selfishness, dissensions, party spirit, envy." All of this constitutes the "works of the flesh."

But with these works, which are undoubtedly evil, Paul contrasts "the fruit of the Spirit," such as "love, joy, peace, patience, kindness, goodness, faithfulness, gentleness, self-control." From the context it is clear that for the Apostle it is not a question of discriminating against and condemning the body, which with the spiritual soul constitutes man's nature and personal subjectivity. Rather, he is concerned with the morally good or bad works, or better the permanent dispositions—virtues and vices—which are the fruit of submission to (in the first case) or of *resistance to* (in the second case) the saving action of the Holy Spirit.

Pope John Paul II, *Dominum et Vivificantem*, (May 18, 1986) no. 55:2-3.

1. Describe the major issue in Galatians 5:1-12.

2. From Galatians 5:6, what is of utmost importance?

> For in ________________ ________________ neither circumcision nor uncircumcision
>
> is of any avail, but ________________ ________________ through __________.

3. How can you attain liberation and salvation? *CCC 1741*

4. What is faith? *CCC 1814*

> ____
>
> ____
>
> ____
>
> ____
>
> ____
>
> ____
>
> ____ *CCC 1814*

5. Can you lose your faith?

1 Timothy 1:18-19	
CCC 162	

6. For what purpose were you called? Galatians 5:13-18

7. How can you keep from falling back into sin? *CCC 2744*

Prayer is a vital necessity ____

____

____

____

____

____

St. John Chrysostom

____

____

________________________________ St. Alphonsus Liguori

8. List 15 works of the flesh. Galatians 5:19-20

9. What is the result of sinful living, catering to the desires of the flesh?

Galatians 5:21	
CCC 1852	

10. What would you say to someone who believes there is no hell, or if there is, no one will go there?

What would Jesus say? Matthew 7:13-14.

11. How could one avoid the end result of sinful living?

1 John 1:8-9	
CCC 1470	

12. Explain the Christian understanding of "concupiscence." *CCC 2515*

13. List 12 fruits of the Spirit. Galatians 5:22-23, *CCC 1832*

14. Circle the one that you would most like to increase. Make a plan to improve in that area.

15. How can you bear more fruit? ***CCC 736***

> By this_______________of the___________________, God's children can bear much fruit.
>
> He who has grafted us onto the true__________will make us__________"the fruit of the
>
> Spirit: … love, _________, peace, ___________, kindness, ____________, faithfulness,
>
> ___________________, self-control." "We live by the ____________"; the more we
>
> ___________________ ourselves, the more we "___________ by the ____________."
>
>   "Through the __________ _____________ we are restored to _______________,
>
> led back to the ________________of _______________, and________________ as
>
> _______________, given __________________ to call God "___________________"
>
> and to_____________in Christ's_______________, called children of _______________
>
> and given a share in ______________________________ _________________." St. Basil
>
>   ***CCC 736***

16. What does Paul instruct in Galatians 5:24-25?

17. What two things does Paul encourage believers to do in Galatians 6:1-2?

18. Compare Galatians 6:7 in two different bible translations and write them below.

19. What will you reap from what you sow? Galatians 6:8

20. What does St. Paul encourage in Galatians 6:9-10?

Jonah & Nahum
Resisting God's Call

Memory Verse

"I called to the Lord, out of my distress, and he answered me."

Jonah 2:2

Nahum and Jonah are two powerful little prophetic books. Even though they are very different, we are placing theme side-by-side because they come from the same moment in Israelite history, centuries before the birth of Christ. At that time, the Assyrians had just destroyed the Northern Kingdom of Israel, carrying away nine of the twelve tribes into captivity. The tribes of Judah, Benjamin and Levi still survived in the Kingdom of Judea, but Assyrian King Sennacherib laid waste to the Judean countryside and besieged Jerusalem. Clearly the Assyrians wanted to wipe God's chosen people off the face of the earth.

Nahum, Prophet of Actual History ~ Nahum remained in Judea, but he preached divine retribution against the Assyrian nation for its historical crimes. Discoveries in Northern Mesopotamia over the past two centuries have given us a very detailed picture of Assyrian culture, and the Book of Nahum can now be appreciated as a magnificently accurate portrayal of Israel's enemy.

(1) The Assyrian rulers bore the title "Shepherd." Nahum knows this, as he writes: "Your shepherds are asleep, O king of Assyria; your nobles slumber. Your people are scattered on the mountains with none to gather them" (Nahum 3:18).

(2) The Assyrian rulers kept domesticated lions in captivity. When dignitaries would come on official state visits, these tame lions would be let loose and hunted for sport. A set of reliefs from the palace of Asshurbanipal in Nineveh portrays the lion hunt, and one magnificent panel shows a dying lioness, her back broken by the spear, collapsed in her death agony. Nahum knows about this sport, and compares the Assyrian rulers to their own hunted lions: "The sword shall devour your young lions" (Nahum 2:13).

(3) The Assyrian rulers decorated their palaces in Nineveh with scenes of battle, including the siege of Lachish in Judea. These panels illustrate the word-pictures painted by our prophet: "The shatterer has come up against you. Man the ramparts, watch the road" (Nahum 2:1). "The chariots rage in the streets, they rush to and fro through the squares; they gleam like torches, they dart like lightning. . . . The river gates are opened, the palace is in dismay" (Nahum 2:4, 6).

History and Poetry ~ *Nahum was a historian, but he was also a poet.* Hebrews tend to state things twice, though the restatement usually displays a slight variation, advancing the thought. Doublets are found everywhere in the Book of Psalms and elsewhere in the poetic and prophetic books of the Hebrew Bible. The entire Book of Nahum consists of prophetic oracles arranged in the doublets typical of Hebrew poetry.

> "Who can stand before his indignation?
> Who can endure the heat of his anger?" (Nahum 1:6).
>
> "The chariots rage in the streets,
> They rush to and fro through the squares" (Nahum 2:4).
>
> "There is no assuaging your hurt,
> Your wound is grievous" (Nahum 3:19).

The Book of Nahum also contains another kind of poetry, the occasional use of allegorical imagery. We have already seen how he uses the images of "shepherd" and "lion" in a culturally accurate but poetic way. Another such parable can be found in chapter three: "All your fortresses are like fig trees with first-ripe figs—if shaken they fall into the mouth of the eater" (Nahum 3:12). Fig trees appear in similar parables elsewhere in the Bible.

Even when biblical authors are most historical, as in the case of Nahum, they remain masterful poets. Other poets, like Jonah, are less interested in historical accuracy and more interested in theological truths.

Jonah, Prophet of Ideal History ~ Jonah describes Nineveh as having repented and been spared. This is not history as it really happened, but history as it should have been and could have been. Jonah describes an ideal Nineveh capable of repentance and forgiveness. Nahum showed us the city that was, while Jonah shows us the city that might have been.

Many people think that God sent prophets to tell us about events that are coming whether we like it or not. This reduces the prophet to nothing but a fortune-teller. True prophets have a much nobler task, to invite people to create a future that would otherwise not come to be. When Isaiah describes the lion lying down with the lamb, this is a vision that we are supposed to help bring into existence. Without our cooperation and our repentance, history will keep on unfolding in its usual way. The prophet shows us how history could be different than it is already.

Within the Book of Nahum, there is only one point of view, which belongs to both God and Nahum. Within the Book of Jonah, however, there are two points of view, God's viewpoint and Jonah's perspective. God wants Jonah to be an instrument of forgiveness, but Jonah wants vengeance. In some ways, perhaps Jonah would have been happier if God had allowed him to do Nahum's job.

Nahum got to stand safely in Judea and preach condemnation against Assyria. God asks Jonah to go to Assyria and preach repentance and forgiveness. If God had asked Nahum to go preach redemption to the Ninevites, Nahum would probably have done exactly what Jonah did—get on a ship headed in the wrong direction, westward toward Tarshish (Spain). As individuals, Nahum and Jonah had exactly the same philosophy towards Nineveh—let it be

destroyed! God lets Nahum persevere in this attitude, but He takes Jonah one step further in moral education to mercy.

God uses Nahum to teach that the God of justice will correct the injustices of history. God uses Jonah to teach that no matter how horrible the crimes of any people or nation, it is never too late for them to repent and be forgiven. These are not contradictory, but complementary truths. Both prophets recognize the reality of injustice in the world, but Jonah's message calls us to a deeper moral growth.

Nahum and Jonah display natural human emotion in wanting God to save Judea and punish the Assyrians. God reveals different attributes of His divine character to these two prophets. Nahum knows a God of justice, while Jonah encounters the God of mercy.

The LORD is a jealous God and avenging, the LORD is avenging and wrathful; The LORD takes vengeance on his adversaries and keeps wrath for his enemies. Nahum 1:2	*I knew that thou art a gracious God and merciful, slow to anger, and abounding in steadfast love, and repentant of evil.* *Jonah 4:2*

Sometimes people say that the God of the Old Testament is a God of vengeance. These people refer to Nahum's understanding of the God of justice. Remember, however, that the Book of Jonah comes from the same part of the Bible, the Old Testament. We must come to appreciate that within the pages of the Hebrew Bible there is a growth in the understanding of the divine nature. Moreover, Christianity is a monotheistic religion. We serve one God. The God of the Old Testament is the same as the God of the New Testament. God defends His chosen people, but He also challenges this people to understand mercy. God does not wait until the coming of Jesus to begin teaching forgiveness. If that were His intention, then Jonah would be located in the New Testament of the Bible, after the coming of Jesus Christ.

Jonah is cited by name nine times in the New Testament. Nahum never receives mention, not even once. Nonetheless, Nahum is not repudiated. Jesus in effect summarizes the theme of Nahum when he says, "All who take the sword will perish by the sword" (Matthew 26:52).

Jonah and the Big Fish ~ Some people seem to get the story of Jonah mixed up with that of Pinocchio. Disney did such a beautiful job of showing Pinocchio's visit to the belly of the whale that we wrongly connect these images with Jonah. Jonah also does something that Pinocchio did not; Jonah sings a psalm to God. The Book of Jonah is largely a prose narrative, except for one large poem towards the middle of the book. At his lowest point, Jonah sings a song not of petition but of thanksgiving! Jonah may have learned this psalm before and found it useful to pray at this point in the narrative. We will see something similar in the Book of Joel, when quoting the psalms becomes a turning point in the prophet's experience. Many lives have similarly been changed through prayer.

Note that Jonah's prayer does not mention the fish. Now, if I had just been rescued by a fish, I would say, "Thank God for the fish!" Jonah, however, does not even seem to notice it. A drowning person might hallucinate and imagine a fish that was not there, or not notice a fish that really was there. Since we were not there, we have no way of knowing whether the fish was real or a vision.

Since Jonah's city of Nineveh is not necessarily a historical city, why should Jonah's fish have been an historical reality? Since Jonah's story upon the land seems to be a parable, couldn't Jonah's story under the sea be a parable, too? The parable of the Good Samaritan is not less inspired because it is a parable rather an historical event.

Christians may attempt to argue and criticize one another over whether Jonah's fish was real; but in so doing, they might miss the whole point of the book. If God could forgive the Assyrians for their crimes against humanity, shouldn't we forgive one another's rigid and uncompromising perceptions of truth?

If Jonah's fish was real, then Hallelujah! But if it was not, then Hallelujah anyway! The fish is an open question in Catholicism. Catholics are free to believe either way about it, and St. Peter will probably not turn anyone away from the pearly gate just because they happen to get the fish question wrong. There are other matters that will be more significant at that time: Have you forgiven those who have wronged you? Do you refuse to forgive someone in your heart?

Even if poetic, Jonah's fish remains important as a foreshadowing of the tomb of Christ. Jesus Himself says, "For as Jonah was three days and three nights in the belly of the whale so will the Son of man be three days and three nights in the heart of the earth" (Matthew 12:40). Jonah was in the fish for 72 hours (three days and three nights), while Christ was in the tomb only 36 hours (two nights with one day in between). So we should not get hung up on details. The enormity and validity of what Christ did in conquering death and rising from the tomb does not depend on the literal historicity of the Jonah account. That would be putting the fish before the tale. The fish gets mentioned in only one verse out of the entire four chapters of the Book of Jonah, and only at the end of chapter one. The fish is not what the Book of Jonah is about, but rather forgiveness. Jonah reveals a glimpse of God, who is gracious and merciful, slow to anger and abounding in steadfast love.

> "He that descended into the subterranean regions came up again. Jesus, who was buried, truly rose again on the third day. Did Jonah come forth from the whale on the third day, and Christ—did He not then come forth from the earth on the third day? Was a dead man raised to life by being touched with the bones of Elisha, and is it not much easier for the Maker of man to be raised by the power of the Father? Well now, He truly rose, and having risen He was seen again by the disciples. Twelve disciples were witnesses to His resurrection, and they did not bear witness with pleasing words, but insisted upon the truth of the resurrection even in the face of torture and death."
> St. Cyril of Jerusalem (315-386 AD), *Catechetical Lectures*, 4,12.

Catholics believe that no sin is so great that it cannot be forgiven in the Sacrament of Penance. We can imagine the notorious sinners of history presenting themselves before a priest, and we know that God's infinite power can forgive even the greatest crimes.

There are some sins that, because of their severity, require more than a simple confession and are reserved for the bishop or the pope. If anyone in America has procured a second abortion, for example, that person must go before the local ordinary before absolution can be given. If a priest has committed an outrage against the Blessed Sacrament or attempted marriage, the confessor must refer these sins to the Sacred Penitentiary in Rome for the assigning of a penance. Mercy and forgiveness await one at the end, but the procedure is more complicated than usual.

Adolf Hitler, Attila the Hun, Judas Iscariot, Mao Tse-Tung, Benito Mussolini or Joseph Stalin could have been forgiven if they repented and cried out for the mercy of God. We see no one excluded from the forgiveness Jesus Christ extends from the Cross, unless he freely chooses to reject the offer of mercy and salvation open to all of mankind.

"Jesus Christ, the Son of the living God, became our reconciliation with the Father. He it was, and He alone, who satisfied the Father's eternal love, that fatherhood that from the beginning found expression in creating the world, giving man all the riches of creation, and making him 'little less than God,' in that he was created 'in the image and after the likeness of God.' He and He alone also satisfied that fatherhood of God and that love which man in a way rejected by breaking the first Covenant and the later covenants that God 'again and again' offered to man. The Redemption of the world—this tremendous mystery of love in which creation is renewed—is, at its deepest root, the fullness of justice in a human heart—the heart of the firstborn Son—in order that it may become justice in the hearts of many human beings, predestined from eternity in the First-born Son to be children of God and called to grace, called to love."

Pope John Paul II, *Redemptor Hominis*, (March 4, 1979) no. 9:1.

Love more powerful than death, more powerful than sin!

"The Cross of Christ, on which the Son, consubstantial with the Father, renders full justice to God, is also a radical revelation of mercy, or rather of the love that goes against what constitutes the very root of evil in the history of man: against sin and death. . . . In the eschatological fulfillment mercy will be revealed as love, while in the temporal phase, in human history, which is at the same time the history of sin and death, love must be revealed above all as mercy and must also be actualized as mercy. Christ's messianic program, the program of mercy, becomes the program of His people, the program of the Church. . . . The Church must consider it one of her principal duties—at every stage of history and especially in our modern age—*to proclaim and to introduce into life* the mystery of mercy, supremely revealed in Jesus Christ. "

Pope John Paul II, *Dives in Misericordia*, (November 13, 1980) no. 8.1, 3, 14.9.

1. Read the short Book of Nahum and write your favorite verse below.

2. Write some attributes of God, or adjectives describing God, from the passages below.

Nahum 1:2	
Nahum 1:3	
Nahum 1:7	

3. How does nature respond to the power of God?   Nahum 1:4-8

4. Why do you think the Lord is so angry? Nahum 1:11-14

5. Compare the following verses.

Isaiah 52:7	
Nahum 1:15	
Romans 10:15	

6. What is the Lord doing?   Nahum 2:2

7. Describe four physical manifestations of desolation in Nahum 2:10.

| |
| |
| |
| |
| |

8. These people are guilty of what sins?   Nahum 3:1-7, 16-19

9. Compare the three devastations in the following two passages.

Nahum 2:13	*Nahum 3:15*

10. Write the following verses below.

Psalm 47:1-3	*Nahum 3:19*

11. Read the short Book of Jonah. Compare the first phrase of Hosea 1:1 with Jonah 1:1.

12. What did God command Jonah to do?   Jonah 1:2

13. How did Jonah respond to God's call?

14. Share a time when you felt the Lord calling you to do something you didn't want to do.

15. What attitudes and emotions can cause man to fail to respond to God's call? *CCC 29*

16. How does Jonah describe himself?   Jonah 1:9

17. Jonah's prayer in Jonah 2:1-9 describes his life and relationship with God. Write a psalm or prayer below that describes your life and your relationship to God.

18. In your own words describe what happened in Jonah chapter 3.

19. What was Jonah's response in Jonah 4:1.

20. What point does Jesus make in using the Jonah analogy in Matthew 12:38-41?

21. To whom does Jesus compare Himself in Luke 11:29-32?

22. How did the people of Nineveh respond and to what result? Luke 11:32.

23. Why should we be merciful and forgiving?   Matthew 6:14-16

24. Explain Jesus' instructions and promises in Luke 6:35-38.

25. Can you think of someone that you have had trouble forgiving, or held a grudge against? Pray for that person this week and ask God to help you to repair or improve the relationship.

Monthly Social Activity

This month your small group will meet for coffee, tea, or a simple breakfast or lunch in someone's home.

Pray for this social event and for the host or hostess. Try if at all possible to attend. Offer hospitality for one of the socials to be held at your home.

Jonah fled from the Lord. Can you think of a time that you felt the Holy Spirit prompting you to do something that you really didn't want to do?

Now reflect on your own present personal life.

- ~ Is there something that the Lord is asking of you?

- ~ Are you fearful, reluctant, eager?

- ~ Ask your group members to help you discern God's call for you.

MICAH 1-2
End of Historical Jerusalem

Memory Verse
**"The LORD is coming forth out of his place,
and will come down and tread upon the high places of the earth.
And the mountains will melt under him and the valleys will be cleft,
like wax before the fire, like waters poured down a steep place."**
MICAH 1:3-4

Meet Micah. The name Micah means "Who Is Like The Lord?" It is synonymous with the name Michael, which means "Who Is Like God?" These are monotheistic names, for they assert the sovereignty and supremacy of the true God of Israel over and above the false gods of the other nations. The Book of Isaiah contains the following statement, an expansion upon the simple question contained in the names Micah and Michael: "'To whom then will you compare me, that I should be like him?' says the Holy One" (Isaiah 40:25).

Micah operated in the southern Kingdom of Judah and commented on the affairs of the northern Kingdom of Israel as it veered toward final collapse. He lived during the reigns of Kings Jotham, Ahaz and Hezekiah (Micah 1:1). The prophet Isaiah operated under these same three kings, and also under the reign of Uzziah before them (Isaiah 1:1). Thus it would seem that Micah was a younger contemporary of Isaiah.

The relationship between Micah and Isaiah is more than just having lived at the same time. Both of these prophets seem to have practiced nudity as a form of lamentation. One of them says: "I will lament and wail; I will go stripped and naked; I will make lamentation like the jackals, and mourning like the ostriches" (Micah 1:8). Similarly, "[M]y servant Isaiah has walked naked and barefoot for three years as a sign and a portent against Egypt and Ethiopia" (Isaiah 20:3).

Among the Jain religionists of India there is an order of priests who go around naked. Apparently there was a movement in ancient Israel that practiced some manner of undress as well, as a kind of prophetic action, indicating the deprivation and lamentation that would befall the country as a result of her failed policies. What is the likelihood of two prophets wandering around Israel in only their loincloths, perhaps, without noticing each other or being part of the same movement? It wasn't a very big country, after all. This shared autobiographical detail suggests that Isaiah and Micah belonged to the same prophetic movement. Micah may have been a disciple of Isaiah, but an important disciple, who achieved a status nearly equal to his teacher's as the latter grew old.

Micah's Inspiration ~ First Isaiah, and then Micah, occupied a leadership role within their prophetic movement. They had inspired words from the Lord, and they were commanded by the Lord (Isaiah 20:2) to execute certain prophetic actions. We can say, then, that there was a quality of inspiration to their entire persons. A true prophet does not give true prophecies one day and false ones the next. Prophecy is not subject to good days and bad days. Rather, the whole sum of the utterance and personal presence of Micah, as of Isaiah, was inspired.

Micah had a ministry from the Lord, and he said many inspired words, only some of which came to be written down in this book. The non-writing prophets may have had few or none of their words written down, but they were inspired in their speech nonetheless. It is important to see that the Book of Micah is not the sum totality of Micah's ministry, but the tip of the iceberg. He said many prophetic and inspired things, and only some of them were written down for posterity. This parallels the apostolic tradition, which is the sum total of the preaching of Peter and the Apostles. It was truly inspired, but only some of it was written down in the pages of the New Testament.

The Acts of the Apostles quotes a portion of Peter's sermon to the crowds on the first Pentecost Sunday. He was filled with the Holy Spirit in every word that he said that day, but only a tiny part is recorded for our enlightenment. Similarly in our day, the exercise of "ex cathedra" infallible pronouncements by the Holy Father is relatively rare—Pope John Paul II has made such statements during his more than 25 years of papacy only in the canonization of over 400 new saints. However, he has issued a new encyclical every year on many different, important subjects, and this is what is called the exercise of the "ordinary magisterium," which is also to be covered implicitly by the protection of infallibility. *In the course of nearly two thousand years, no pope acting in his capacity as teacher of the faithful has ever made even one doctrinally false statement!*

Micah, as a true prophet of the Lord, was inspired in the totality of his ministry, just as the popes have been infallible not just in each doctrinal definition but in a general way. The popes are successors of the apostles — and the apostles in a certain sense are successors of Jesus and of the prophets. The Holy Spirit has spread a blanket of inspiration over all their work in the first instance, and a blanket of infallibility in the second instance.

Micah's Rural Point of View ~ Micah came from the little village of Moresheth (Micah 1:1). Arriving in the big city, he was horrified by the corruption and sinfulness that he found there. This perspective was not unique among the prophets of Israel. The prophet Nahum came from the otherwise unknown village of Elkosh (Nahum 1:1). Amos, too, had been a rural person—"I am no prophet nor a prophet's son; but I am a herdsman, and a dresser of sycamore trees, and the LORD took me from following the flock, and the LORD said to me, 'Go, prophesy to my people Israel' " (Amos 7:14).

The injustices and vices that the prophets of Israel condemned were those that typically flourish in urban settings—prostitution, thievery, unfair labor practices, and religious indifference and apostasy. When Joshua led the twelve tribes of Israel into the Promised Land, they had been nomadic and semi-agrarian peoples. Slowly they settled in the cities of Canaan, and in the process, entered into urban temptations. Their all-too-ready acceptance of all that was worst, as well as what was best, in urban living provided all the prophets with sermon material. Eventually, Judaism and Christianity would come to terms with city life and learn how to thrive there, but it took time for the monotheistic tradition to move from the cocoon of tribal living to the cosmopolitan atmosphere.

Micah lived at an early stage in this shift of setting. Soon, during the Exile, the people of God would have to make a nearly complete break with their agrarian past. The post-exilic prophets will have to challenge them to make a future in the cities. Micah has a much more

conservative mentality. His whole message is infused with this culture shock that came as a result of his move to the city.

Micah's book contains the interesting statement: "What is the transgression of Jacob? Is it not Samaria? And what is the sin of the house of Judah? Is it not Jerusalem?" (Micah 1:5). Samaria, of course, is the metropolis of the Northern Kingdom, and Jerusalem the metropolis of the Southern. It is as if someone today were to write, "What is the sin of England? It is London. What is the sin of France? It is Paris." Or, "What is the sin of the United States? It is Washington, D.C." We can immediately understand that the governments that function from those capital cities are the source of the problem. Hence, Micah is clearly pointing a finger at the ruling class of the Northern and Southern Kingdoms, but also at the vices that flourish in those urban settings.

Of course, Micah does not mean to exempt the rest of the country from blame. Rather, he uses the capital city as a kind of poetic symbol for the country as a whole. This is the poetic figure of speech technically called "synecdoche," the substitution of the part for the whole. The capital city is only a part of the country, after all, but we frequently name the capital when we mean the whole country, as when we say "Berlin" to mean Germany, or "Moscow" when we mean Russia.

Even so, Micah makes a distinction between the fate of the large cities and that of the smaller settlements. He says that the inhabitants of Lachish, the largest fortress city in Judah, will give parting gifts to their country cousins in his own hometown of Moresheth-gath, when they are carried away in captivity. Lachish was besieged by the Assyrians, and a wall relief of that siege decorated the Northwest Palace of Ashurbanipal in the Assyrian capital of Nineveh. In the 19th Century, British archaeologists took that relief to the British Museum in London, where it is on display to this day. There one can see the prophecy of Micah fulfilled.

Since, according to Micah, the small towns will not suffer as devastating a fate as the large cities, the future survival of the Israelite people depends upon the rural folk. So, in his final vision later in the book, Micah will write: "But you, O Bethlehem Ephratha, who are little to be among the clans of Judah, from you shall come forth for me one who is to be ruler in Israel, whose origin is from of old, from ancient days" (Micah 5:2). The sages of Israel quoted this passage to indicate their expectation that the Messiah would be born not in Jerusalem, the great city, but in the small town of Bethlehem (Matthew 2:6). Many baby boys will die in the slaughter of the innocents because of Herod's futile attempt to prevent this prophecy from being fulfilled.

Micah's Audiences ~ The first oracle of Micah is addressed to the entire world: "Hear, you peoples, all of you; hearken, O earth, and all that is in it" (Micah 1:2). Of course the whole world will not receive this message, because the prophet is not going to travel around the world to deliver it. Here we have the figure of speech called "apostrophe," when a speaker addresses an inanimate object or someone not present. When an atheist says, "O my god!" it is that kind of language; he doesn't think anybody is really listening to his remark.

Micah's intended audience is not the entire world, but the Israelites who were listening to his message. It is for their benefit that he utters the prophecy. He means to warn the Israelites about the nations of the world who are coming to harm them. So his expressed audience is not the same as his intended audience.

One day, however, the Christian apostles will carry the Book of Micah to the whole world. Then the audience that Micah intended only as a figure of speech will become a real audience, when people throughout the world read his book and learn from its prophecies. At that time, the Holy Spirit who is the divine author of Micah's book extends the importance and significance of Micah's audience to a real, worldwide scale. The audience that Micah never expected to hear his message will hear it, because the apostles will take the Word of God to the ends of the earth.

Micah is a book, then, with two authors and two audiences. The two authors are the Holy Spirit and Micah; the two audiences are the Israelites and the whole world. Micah is only really talking to the Israelites; whereas, the Holy Spirit speaks both to them and to the whole world.

So, the urban evils that Micah condemns within the Kingdoms of Israel and of Judah are repulsive to the Holy Spirit everywhere in the world. The prophetic challenge to sane and just living is not just a provincial message for the chosen people, but a universal message to all peoples on the face of the earth. The Old Testament prophets addressed their message to one people, while the apostles have the charge of expanding the same message in a larger form to the whole world.

Called to salvation through faith in Jesus Christ, "the true lights that enlightens everyone" (John 1:9), people become "light in the Lord" and "children of light" (Ephesians 5:8), and are made holy by "obedience to the truth" (1 Peter 1:22).

This obedience is not always easy. As a result of that mysterious original sin, committed at the prompting of Satan, the one who is a "liar and the father of lies" (John 8:44). Man's capacity to know the truth is also darkened, and his will to submit to it is weakened. Thus, giving himself over to relativism and skepticism, he goes off in search of an illusory freedom apart from truth itself.

But, no darkness of error or of sin can totally take away from man the light of God the Creator. In the depths of his heart there always remains a yearning for absolute truth and a thirst to attain full knowledge of it. This is eloquently proved by man's tireless search for knowledge in all fields. It is proved even more by his search for the *meaning of life*. The development of science and technology, this splendid testimony of the human capacity for understanding and for perseverance, does not free humanity from the obligations to ask the ultimate religious questions. Rather, it spurs us on to face the most painful and decisive of struggles, those of the heart and of the moral conscience.

No one can escape from the fundamental questions: *What must I do? How do I distinguish good from evil?* The answer is only possible thanks to the splendor of the truth which shines forth deep within the human spirit, as the Psalmist bears witness: "There are many who say: 'O that we might see some good! Let the light of your face shine on us, O Lord'" (Psalm 4:6).

Pope John Paul II, *Veritatis Splendor*, (August 6, 1993) no.1.1 - 2.1.

1. What will happen when the Lord comes? Micah 1:2-4

2. For what sins, will the Lord come? Micah 1:5-7

3. How will the prophet Micah respond to the sins of the people? Micah 1:8-9

4. Identify some signs of mourning for sin and repentance from Micah 1:10-16.

5. Discuss some ways in which contemporary society deals with sin.

  ___ Denial   ___ Blame

  ___ Rationalization   ___ Making excuses

  ___ Other, please explain

6. What can modern day Christians do to deal with sin?

Matthew 11:28-29	
Acts 3:19	
CCC 1421	
CCC 1425	

7. Compare the following verses.

Micah 2:1-4	
Psalm 36:4	
Isaiah 5:8-12	
Isaiah 32:7	
Amos 8:4	
Sirach 2:12-14	

8. How does the Catholic Church view human woes? *CCC 2448*

"In its various forms—_________________ _____________________, unjust _________________, physical and psychological illness and death—_______________ _______________ is the obvious sign of the inherited condition of frailty and __________ for _________________ in which man finds himself as a consequence of _____________ __________. This misery elicited the _________________ of _________________ the _____________________, who _____________________ took it upon himself and _____________________ himself with the _________________ of the brethren. Hence, those who are oppressed by poverty are the object of a _____________________ _______________ on the part of the _______________ which, since her origin and in spite of the _____________________ of many of her members, has not ceased to work for their _______________, _______________, and liberation through numerous __________ of _________________ which remains indispensable always and everywhere. *CCC 2448*

9. Describe the situation in Micah 2:6-11.

10. Name two or three modern day prophets or preachers.

11. Have you ever felt confused, listening to the voices of conflicting preachers?

12. How can you figure out whose teaching is true? *CCC 2034*

CCC 2034

13. In the midst of confusion and conflict, what should be the role of your conscience?
     CCC 2039

14. What charism preserves and explains the saving truths of the faith? *CCC 2035*

15. Describe the preacher in Micah 2:11.

16. Can you think of a preacher who was attractive for saying what people wanted to hear?

17. What hope and promise is offered in Micah 2:12-14?

18. What means does God use to keep his flock gathered together in truth? *CCC 1548*

In the ecclesial service of the ordained minister, _________________________

____

____

____

____. *CCC 1548*

19. Why has the sacrament of Holy Orders been instituted? *CCC 1551*

20. What two tasks does the priest have? *CCC 1552*

21. Choose one of the following practical applications to do this week and then do it!

_______ *Pray for the pope.*

_______ *Read a papal encyclical.*

_______ *Pray for your bishop.*

_______ *Pray for your parish priest.*

_______ *Thank your priest for ministering to you.*

_______ *Bake something for your pastor.*

_______ *Spend time in Adoration praying for vocations.*

_______ *Write to encourage or thank a seminarian, priest or bishop.*

MICAH 3-7
Rise of Spiritual Jerusalem

Memory Verse

"He has showed you, O man, what is good; and what does the LORD require of you but to do justice, and to love kindness, and to walk humbly with your God?"

MICAH 6:8

The prophets experienced persecution because of their message. People said: "'Do not preach'—thus they preach—'one should not preach of such things; disgrace will not overtake us'" (Micah 2:6). When people hear a message that they do not want to hear, they will sometimes shoot the messenger. Jeremiah found himself thrown into a well by an unreceptive audience. Ten of the twelve original apostles found themselves martyred by the peoples to whom the Lord had sent them. One never speaks the Word of the Lord out of desire for personal profit, because the consequences are so frequently deleterious.

Nonetheless, Micah's message is not one of doom but one of liberation. We do not have to be enslaved to sin. God cares for us and is reaching down to save us. So Micah, despite living in a time of impending destruction, has a consoling aspect to his message: "I will surely gather all of you, O Jacob, I will gather the remnant of Israel; I will set them together like sheep in a fold" (Micah 2:12).

Those who would exercise the gift of prophecy without actually having received any message from the Lord face two pitfalls on either side of them:
— one is to deliver nothing but gloom,
    because, no matter how good things are, they are bound to get worse eventually;
— the other is to deliver a message of false hope,
    because that is what people want to hear.

The Lord gives Micah an oracle against the false prophets, and says that "it shall be night to you, without vision, and darkness to you, without divination. The sun shall go down upon the [false] prophets, and the day shall be black over them; the seers shall be disgraced, and the diviners put to shame" (Micah 3:6).

False prophecy is a form of superstition. Those who use astrology, tarot cards or Ouija boards receive messages that are not from the Lord but from occult spirits. Don't play with fire and risk the danger of putting yourself into the power of Satan by toying with spiritualist mediums. A wise Christian will avoid such practices scrupulously! The gift of faith must not be abused, because faith is too precious a gift to be jeopardized in such a way. As the Lord prophesies that the false prophets will lose their sight, those who seek spiritual insight through

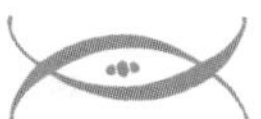

false means can lose the little insight they have. The devil, the father of lies, knows nothing but what God allows him to know, and we can get more accurate information directly from the Almighty than through lying intermediaries.

Micah and Isaiah ~ There is an extensive passage in Micah 4:1-3 that is found word-for-word in Isaiah 2:2-4. These words are identical in both prophetic books:

It shall come to pass in the latter days
that the mountain of the house of the LORD
shall be established as the highest of the mountains,
and shall be raised up above the hills;
and peoples shall flow to it,
and many nations shall come, and say:
'Come, let us go up to the mountain of the LORD,
to the house of the God of Jacob;
that he may teach us his ways
and we may walk in his paths.'
For out of Zion shall go forth the law,
and the word of the LORD from Jerusalem.
He shall judge between many peoples,
and shall decide for strong nations afar off;
and they shall beat their swords into plowshares,
and their spears into pruning hooks;
nation shall not lift up sword against nation,
neither shall they learn war any more.
(Isaiah 2:2-4, Micah 4:1-4)

This very important prophecy promises the ultimate victory of peace over war. It is related to the beautiful Isaiah prophecy about the lion lying down with the lamb. One would be tempted to think that Micah, who was younger, had borrowed this prophecy from Isaiah. The matter may be more complicated than that. For one thing, Isaiah breaks off the oracle before Micah does. Micah continues: "but they shall sit every man under his vine and under his fig tree, and none shall make them afraid; for the mouth of the LORD of hosts has spoken" (Micah 4:4). This seems not to be an addendum, but an integral part of the oracle. It provides a typical prophetic conclusion, with the statement "for the mouth of the LORD of hosts has spoken."

If Micah did not copy Isaiah, because he has the fuller form of the prophecy, then could it be that Isaiah copied Micah? Can a teacher copy the work of his disciple? Stranger things have happened, and this is not out of the realm of possibility. Or, the Holy Spirit could have inspired each of these prophets individually, as God sometimes delivers the same message to several people.

What is the actual relationship between these two prophets, then? It is likely that Micah was a disciple in the school of Isaiah, but an important disciple. It may be that, after the death of Isaiah, Micah had a hand in assembling an early form of the Book of Isaiah, as well as the editing of his own prophetic book under his own name. In later generations, Isaiah's book continued to grow, but Micah's book was fixed in its original form. At a certain point in the expansion of Isaiah's book, Micah's prophecy came to be assimilated to the official version of his master's book.

Micah and Jeremiah ~ Most of Micah's prophecy has to do with the doom impending upon the Northern Kingdom, but at the end of chapter 3 there is a prophecy about the fate of Jerusalem:

> Therefore because of you
> Zion shall be plowed as a field;
> Jerusalem shall become a heap of ruins,
> and the mountain of the house a wooded height.
> (Micah 3:12)

This passage, somewhat unique to Micah, attracts the attention of the prophet Jeremiah, who quotes it in its entirety at his trial over a hundred years later:

> And certain elders of the land arose and spoke to all the assembled people, saying:
> Micah of Moresheth prophesied in the days of Hezekiah king of Judah,
> and said to all the people of Judah:
> 'Thus says the LORD of hosts,
> Zion shall be plowed as a field;
> Jerusalem shall become a heap of ruins,
> and the mountain of the house a wooded height.'
> (Jeremiah 26:17-18)

It is clear from this passage that Micah, though belonging to the school of Isaiah, was fully accepted by the Jeremiah school as a true prophet of the Lord. It is also clear that the Book of Micah already was fully accepted as an inspired book. His is the only prophecy quoted in defense of Jeremiah at his trial.

God's Own Lament ~ A very moving passage in the Book of Micah is the Lord's *improperia*, or lamentation against his people. The more correct translation of "improperia" is "complaint." Therefore, we can prayerfully meditate on these very piercing words, pondering God's complaint against his people:

> O my people, what have I done to you?
> In what have I wearied you? Answer me!
> For I brought you up from the land of Egypt,
> and redeemed you from the house of bondage.
> (Micah 6:3-4)

This passage is quite similar to that in Isaiah 5, where the Lord invites the Jerusalemites to judge between Him and His vineyard: "For the vineyard of the LORD of hosts is the house of Israel" (Isaiah 5:7).

For more than a millennium the Lord's lament from Micah formed part of the liturgy of Good Friday. The Church understood Jesus to be lamenting the treatment that He was receiving during His Passion. Of course, good Christians saw in these words not a condemnation of the Jews but an indictment for their own sins, which had made necessary the sufferings of the Redeemer. Unfortunately, not a few anti-Semites seized upon these

sentiments as justification for their views. There sadly are documented cases of worshippers leaving church on Good Friday and going into the ghetto to attack their Jewish neighbors. One such incident is recounted in the thirteenth-century Cantigas of Santa Maria published by the Crown of Spain.

It is to the credit of the Jewish Scriptures that they contain an honest appraisal of Jewish failings. What other nation has so accurately described its own faults? This is the great tradition behind the Christian examination of conscience. We have learned from our Jewish forebears in the faith that one must take honest stock of one's own soul in order to appear before the Lord.

To blame the historical Jews for the sufferings of Christ, which my own sins made theologically necessary, cheapens and distorts the whole meaning of the redemption. In the face of Jesus' great mercy, "Father, forgive them for they know not what they do" (Luke 23:24), each of us must humbly accept mercy without condemning others. Because some Christians have taken Micah's beautiful words out of their spiritual context, the rest of us are deprived of the benefit of hearing them on Good Friday. Shame on those who blame the Jews for the sufferings that we have all caused Christ. Shame and more shame.

God's Forgiveness ~ The Book of Micah ends with a prophecy of forgiveness:

> He will again have compassion upon us,
> he will tread our iniquities under foot.
> Thou wilt cast all our sins
> into the depths of the sea.
> (Micah 7:19)

This prophecy began to be fulfilled on Good Friday when our Lord paid the price for our ransom from sin, but the prophecy is only completely fulfilled when we receive this forgiveness into our souls in the sacraments of the church. What a balm in Gilead it is to hear sacramental absolution pronounced over us! Too many Catholics fear or neglect to go to Confession and tell the sins that can be "cast into the depths of the sea" by these simple words:

God the Father of mercies through the death and resurrection of His Son
has reconciled the world to Himself
and sent the Holy Spirit among us for the forgiveness of sin.
Through the ministry of the church
may the Lord grant you pardon and peace,
and I absolve you of your sins
in the Name of the Father and of the Son and of the Holy Spirit.
Amen.

1. Who is accused in Micah 3:1-3 and for what misdeeds?

2. Compare the following verses.

Isaiah 5:20	
Micah 3:2	

3. What will happen to the leaders when they cry out? Micah 3:4-10

4. Find common threads in the following passages.

Amos 5:6-7	
Micah 4:9-12	
Habakkuk 2:12	

5. What will happen in the latter days? Micah 4:1-3

6. Uncover the hope found in the following passages.

Micah 4:3-4	
Zechariah 3:10	

7. Prophets accuse Israel of breaking the covenant. This is in preparation for what? *CCC 762*

8. What does the Lord promise in the following verses?

Micah 4:6-8	
Isaiah 40:9-11	
Ezekiel 34:11-16	
Zephaniah 3:19-20	
John 10:7-16	

9. What is foretold in these passages?

Isaiah 48:20	
Isaiah 52:11-12	
Micah 4:9-10	

10. Identify the significance of the places mentioned in these passages.

Genesis 35:19	
Ruth 4:11	
1 Samuel 17:12	
Micah 5:2	
Luke 2:4-7	

11. What is foretold in Micah 5:2-6?

12. Explain what the remnant of Jacob will be.   Micah 5:7-9

13. What will be done in the following verses?

Micah 5:10-15	
Zechariah 9:10	
Exodus 34:13-14	

14. Explain the following passages in your own words.

Numbers 22:1-6	
Numbers 25:1-5	
Joshua 4:19-24	
Isaiah 3:12-13	
Hosea 4:1-3	
Micah 6:1-7	

15. What three things does the Lord require of you?   Micah 6:8

Micah 6:8	*to do justice*	Amos 5:24
Micah 6:8		Hosea 2:19-20
Micah 6:8		Matthew 23:23

16. In which of the above would you like to improve? How can you work on it? Be practical.

17. Describe the complaints of the Lord and the judgments to come. Micah 6:9-16

Complaints	**Judgments**

18. Explain the situation in Micah 7:1-7. Where is the corruption?

19. What will God do from Micah 7:8-20?

20. Compare the following verses.

Micah 7:6		Matthew 10:35
Micah 7:10		Psalm 79:10
Micah 7:14		Jeremiah 50:19
Micah 7:20		Luke 1:54-55

BARUCH 1-2
Prophecy in Exile

Memory Verse

**"Righteousness belongs to the Lord our God,
but confusion of face, as at this day, to us …
because we have sinned before the Lord, and have disobeyed him,
and have not heeded the voice of the Lord our God,
to walk in the statutes of the Lord which he set before us."**

BARUCH 1:15,17-18

pen your Bible to the Book of Baruch and you will find one of three things:

1) Baruch is found after the Prophet Jeremiah and Lamentations, where he belongs, or
2) Baruch is located in an appendix after the New Testament, or
3) There is no Baruch to be found anywhere!

If Baruch is not in your Bible, then your Bible in not adequate for Catholic use, and you should seriously consider getting a complete one. This leads to the question of why Baruch—and six other books of the Catholic Bible—are not to be found in Protestant editions. At some point, not necessarily in the generation of the original Reformers but perhaps within a century, these books were excluded for the simple reason that they were not found in the Hebrew Bible used by Jews of their day.

That leads to the next question, why did the Jews not include these books? The early rabbis came to their conclusion about which books to include in the Hebrew Bible at about the same time that the early bishops were discerning the canon of Sacred Scripture. The rabbis and the bishops did not consult with each other. They both had at their disposal a large body of writings, some of which was the inspired Word of God and some of which was not. The bishops came up with a slightly larger "canon" of scripture than the rabbis did.

As Catholics, we believe that the Holy Spirit guided the early bishops infallibly in their decision about which books to include in the Bible. The editors of the Protestant Bibles chose to follow the Jewish rather than the ancient Christian tradition about the canon of Scripture. It is difficult to justify their decision from a theological point of view, since Jesus entrusted such matters to Peter and his successors, rather than to anyone else. Some of the Dead Sea Scrolls discovered after World War II were the original Hebrew texts for several of the so-called "apocryphal" or "deutero-canonical" books. The Dead Sea Scrolls prove that these are authentic ancient Jewish writings and not ecclesiastical fabrications.

At a public lecture in Jerusalem on July 29, 1975, Professor Raphael Jehudah Zwi Werblowsky, a prominent Jewish historian from the Hebrew University, thanked the Catholic Church for saving these ancient writings. He said that without the help of the Church, the Jewish people would have lost several centuries of their history. The scribe Baruch adds an important dimension to our understanding of the early period of the Jewish exile in Babylon, for example.

Meet Baruch the Scribe (Jeremiah 36). We know more about the prophet Baruch than about any of the other twelve "minor" prophets, because he is mentioned prominently in the Book of Jeremiah. As a matter of fact, we learn in chapter 36 of that book that Baruch was the scribe who wrote down the book of the sayings of Jeremiah. Jeremiah, it seems, was illiterate, because when the word of the Lord told Jeremiah to write down his prophecies, the first thing Jeremiah does is summon the scribe Baruch: "[A]nd Baruch wrote upon a scroll at the dictation of Jeremiah all the words of the LORD which He had spoken to him" (Jeremiah 36:4).

Baruch, the Scribe ~ Then Jeremiah sent Baruch to the temple to read aloud the scroll that he had written for him. Jeremiah offers this excuse for not going himself: "I am debarred from going to the house of the LORD, so you are to go" (Jeremiah 36:5). Now it may very well be that Jeremiah was not allowed at that time to enter the temple, but this also sounds very much like the kind of excuse that an unlettered person knows how to use to avoid a situation that will reveal his inability to read or write. If Jeremiah could not write his own scroll, it is very likely that he could not read his own scroll, either.

Jeremiah is usually listed among the "writing prophets" because he has his own book, while Elijah is listed among the "non-writing prophets" because only fragments of his prophecies are found in the historical books. We see here, however, that the distinction between writing and non-writing prophets rather breaks down. Some of the "non-writing prophets" may have been personally literate, while some of the "writing prophets" may have been illiterate.

At the time of the prophets and even of the apostles, literacy was a relatively rare and specialized phenomenon. Only a tiny percentage of the total population could read and write, and for many of those it provided the means of their livelihood. Most of the people depended upon professional scribes to draw up their legal documents, and perform other services of the like. Even the wealthy and powerful had servants to do their paperwork for them.

In the same chapter of Jeremiah it very much appears that King Jehoiakim and his court are unable to read: "Then the king sent Jehudi to get the scroll, and he took it from the chamber of Elishama the secretary; and Jehudi read it to the king and all the princes who stood beside the king" (Jeremiah 36:21). This Jehudi was the king's scribe, just as Baruch was the prophet's scribe. Both kings and prophets depended upon others to do their writing and their reading for them. That was just the way things were in those days.

Most people then relied more on memory than we do today. Poets, historians, philosophers, and teachers of all subjects, committed their texts to memory themselves, and used rote learning as a means of transmitting this cultural material to their students. The prophets had disciples, who memorized the saying of their masters. Similarly, Jesus transmitted His sayings to His followers, the apostles. Eventually some of these things got written down and became The Book. The preaching itself of the prophets and apostles is larger than the written record, and the quality of inspiration belongs to the whole process, not just of the fragmentary result.

Within the small course of this one chapter, poor Jeremiah has to dictate the whole book not once, but twice. The king expresses symbolically, even ritualistically, his utter contempt

for Jeremiah and his messages by destroying the first manuscript. "As Jehudi read three or four columns, the king would cut them off with his penknife and throw them into the fire in the brazier, until the entire scroll was consumed" (Jeremiah 36:23). Now the king was destroying the Word of the Lord, as given through the prophet Jeremiah, but he was physically burning the handiwork of the scribe Baruch. Then Jeremiah had to dictate a second edition of his book to the scribe Baruch to write again.

Now a manuscript was an expensive item in those days. The parchment was specially treated lambskin, and the ink was an expensive commodity as well. Jeremiah was investing some large portion of personal resources into committing his book to writing, and the expense was now double because he had to dictate a second copy. No doubt Baruch had to be paid also. The scribe's work was indispensable, and he had to receive a stipend commensurate with his professional status. The fee for reading a work aloud as Jehudi did would be fairly small, but the fee for writing a work down as Baruch did would be very large. It would be nice to think of Baruch as offering his services to Jeremiah free of charge, out of loyalty to the prophet. If Baruch were one of Jeremiah's disciples, he might have done so.

Interestingly, the second edition of Jeremiah's book ends up longer than the first, because there is a new prophecy added: "and many similar words were added to them" (Jeremiah 36:32). We are privileged to see here in the Book of Jeremiah chapter 36, more than anywhere else, a description of the actual process of biblical composition, which may have varied from book to book.

We also see that the scribe Baruch is responsible for putting down in writing two books that appear in our Old Testament—his own book, and the Book of Jeremiah. Similarly, it may be that the prophet Micah was responsible for writing down both his own book and that of Isaiah (since there is a prophecy contained with identical wording in both books). Similarly, in the New Testament, Luke writes down a Gospel containing the parables and sayings of Jesus, but he also writes his own book, the Acts of the Apostles. In each of these cases, the scribe functions as a ghost-writer for someone else, and then steps forward to produce a work in his own name.

Baruch's Ancestry ~ In the Book of Jeremiah, Baruch is known simply as "Baruch the son of Neriah" (Jeremiah 36:4). At the beginning of his own book, however, Baruch gives himself a much longer genealogy. "These are the words of the book which Baruch, the son of Neraiah, son of Mahseiah, son of Zedekiah, son of Hasadiah, son of Hilkiah, wrote in Babylon" (Baruch 1:1).

Baruch the secretary is now becoming Baruch the author. He wants to make it perfectly clear that this is his own book, and so he gives the full form of his name, tracing back his ancestry six generations. Perhaps several of those ancestors were famous scribes themselves in their day, since a profession of this sort would have been handed down from father to son. He establishes his authority by citing famous ancestors, know by reputation to his readership.

We meet Baruch's brother elsewhere—Seraiah the son of Neriah, son of Mahseiah: "Seraiah was the quartermaster" (Jeremiah 51:59). Now the quartermaster would have to have the skills of a scribe. So we learn that there are two scribes in Baruch's family in the same generation. It must run in the family.

Just as Jehudi had read the book of Jeremiah to the king of Jerusalem, so Baruch reads his own book to the crown prince of Judah, in his place of exile "in Babylon by the river Sud. Then they wept" (Baruch 1:4-5). Baruch calls Babylon's river by the name Sud, while the Greeks called the same river the Euphrates. Most other important cities of Mesopotamia stood along the banks of the Tigris instead—Nineveh, and modern-day, Bagdad. Here, Baruch reminds us of that psalm of exile.

> By the waters of Babylon, there we sat down and wept, when we remembered Zion.
> On the willows there we hung up our lyres.
> For there our captors required of us songs, and our tormentors, mirth, saying,
> "Sing us one of the songs of Zion!"
> How shall we sing the LORD's song in a foreign land?
> If I forget you, O Jerusalem, let my right hand wither!
> Let my tongue cleave to the roof of my mouth, if I do not remember you,
> if I do not set Jerusalem above my highest joy!
> Psalm 137:1-6

The Role of the Scribe ~ Notice that by reading to the crown prince, Baruch seems to have risen in social standing. Whereas before he was merely the scribe of an unpopular prophet, now he has taken the place of the king's own scribe in the social pecking order of the Judeans in exile. The nation has been smashed, the elite swept away into exile, the royalty overturned, but the scribe has risen in significance. During Baruch's own lifetime a catastrophic change has befallen the people, but new institutions are arising to take the place of those that have been destroyed. The Era of the Monarchy has ended, and now begins the Era of the Scribe.

Scribes will make it possible for the Jewish people to survive in exile, by writing down their customs for transmission to later generations. The very existence of the Bible is a result of the literary activity of the scribes among the People of God. While they were in their own land, the architecture, social institutions, geography, and even the weather, could remind them of God's promises. Now that they are no longer in their land, they need the work of the scribes to give them cultural cohesion.

How many scribes will fulfill important roles in the coming centuries of Jewish history? The scribe Ezra will lead the people back to Jerusalem after the end of the exile. The scribe Sirach will put the finishing touches on the wisdom tradition. The scribes in Jesus' day will hold the key to the people's identity, and some of those scribes will become evangelists. Scribes will write down the stories of the great rabbis, which becomes the rabbinic literature that is at the basis of modern Judaism. After the destruction of the second temple, the role of the priesthood will shrink, but that of the scribes will grow accordingly. If Jews and Christians are "People of the Book," as Moslems call them, then the scribes are the people who are responsible for writing down and copying and preserving the Book. It was during the lifetime of Baruch that the position of scribe began to be elevated. In the first part of his career he was a paid scribbler, but in the second part he became a biblical author.

1. To whom did Baruch read the words of his book?   Baruch 1:1-4

2. Where were Baruch and the people at that time? Baruch 1:4

3. How did the people respond to Baruch's words?   Baruch 1:5-9

4. Who was the high priest in Jerusalem at that time? Baruch 1:5-7

5. Compare the following verses.

Jeremiah 24:1	
Baruch 1:9	

6. Can you find a fulfillment of Jeremiah's prophecy in the following verse?

Jeremiah 29:7	
Baruch 1:11	

7. Find three things that the people pray for or hope for in Baruch 1:12

8. Describe what is happening in Baruch 1:13-14.

9. What should you do to deal with sin? *CCC 1847*

"God created us without us: but he did not will to save us without us." ________________

____

____

____

____

____

____

____. *CCC 1847*

10. Compare the following verses. What do they tell you about God?

Baruch 1:15-16	
Baruch 2:6-8	

11. Can you recall a time in your life when you were given a warning that you did not heed?

12. Compare the following verses.

Daniel 9:7-10	
Baruch 1:18	

13. Identify some warnings in the following passages.

Leviticus 26:14-39	
Deuteronomy 28:15-38	
Baruch 1:20-22	

14. Can you guess what the sin of the people might have been?

15. Read Baruch 6 (The Letter of Jeremiah) and list the verses that suggest their sin.

16. For further help, look up Idolatry in the Catechism. *CCC 2112*

The first commandment condemns _______________________________________

____

____

____

____

____

____

____

____

____.   *CCC 2112*

17. List as many "contemporary idols" as you can think of that tempt people today.

18. What is the best way to avoid the sin of idolatry in your own life?

BARUCH 3-6
Act of Contrition

Memory Verse

**"O Lord Almighty, God of Israel,
the soul in anguish and the wearied spirit cry out to thee.
Hear, O Lord, and have mercy,
for we have sinned before thee."**

BARUCH 3:1-2

Act of Contrition ~ Baruch 1:15-3:8 comprises one of the longest prayers in the whole Bible, a great prayer of amendment to God for the sins which brought disaster upon the people. Baruch exempts God from any blame and places the whole responsibility for the present troubles upon the people themselves. This corresponds with the great biblical tradition.

The Greeks and other ancient people believed in gods who were whimsical, treating the nations of the earth like putty in their hands. When disaster struck, the moody gods were to blame. Ultimately, human beings had no freedom and no destiny, and were not responsible for their actions, except insofar as they may have inadvertently angered a god, as Paris did when he spurned the goddess Athena, for example, by choosing the human woman Helen over the goddess. This behavior resulted in the Trojan War and disaster for Troy.

Hebrew theology exempts God from blame for human history, and places the full responsibility on the people themselves for their own actions and the consequences of those actions. The Hebrew God sends prophets to direct the people in the right path, so that they may avoid danger and distress. If the Hebrew people stray, God helps them back to Himself. If they persist in going off the deep end, however, they are free to choose disaster. As Moses said to the people: "I call heaven and earth to witness against you this day, that I have set before you life and death, blessing and curse; therefore choose life, that you and your descendants may live" (Deuteronomy 30:19).

Suffering the punishments for sin, Jewish kings and priests, scribes and people implore the Lord for forgiveness by claiming the guilt for themselves and exonerating God Himself from any blame. *Today, people blame God, society, history, genetics, parents, teachers, ethnicity, drugs, alcohol, gender, anything but themselves, for their problems!* This is not the biblical way.

In the great Catholic tradition, the true penitent examines his or her conscience every evening before bed, to determine whether there has been any offense against God or fellow man that day. It is amazing how quickly the well-formed Catholic conscience can find a blemish in the day's performance, and how a firm purpose of amendment rises quickly in the Catholic heart. So many people on the earth seem to lack the ability to recognize or admit their own faults. Our readiness to see our failings is a great heritage received from the Jews.

Catholics memorize a prayer of contrition to recite during the sacrament of Confession, before the priest gives absolution. There are different forms of the Act of Contrition, traditional and modern, longer and shorter. One would wager that no Catholic has ever memorized the Act of Contrition found in the Book of Baruch and attempted to recite it in the Confessional. In fact, because of the prayer's great length, the priest might even grow impatient—not to mention the line of penitents waiting outside. Nonetheless, this prayer contains passages of great beauty and heartfelt expressions of sorrow. "[W]e have sinned, we have been ungodly, we have done wrong, O Lord our God, against all thy ordinances. Let thy anger turn away from us" (Baruch 2:12-13a).

As Baruch and the people prayed for forgiveness in their Babylonian exile, so we here, in our earthly exile, this vale of tears, as sojourners and wayfarers upon the earth, pray for the divine forgiveness that will reopen to us the gates of paradise.

The name Baruch means "Blessed," appearing in Jewish ritual blessings, which often say "Blessed be God," or "Blessed be the Lord." We usually think of blessing as something that God does for us, but in our Judaeo-Christian prayer tradition we can also speak about our blessing God. He, of course, does not need our blessing, but when we bless Him, we ourselves are blessed.

When the Old Testament speaks about a man or woman being "blessed," most of the time a different Hebrew word is used, the word "Asher." So the blessing of God uses "Baruch" while the blessing of a human being uses "Asher." Compare the first verses of Psalm 1 and Psalm 144.

Blessed *(ASHER)* is the man who walks not in the counsel of the wicked, nor stands in the way of sinners, nor sits in the seat of scoffers. (Psalm 1:1)	Blessed *(BARUCH)* be the LORD, my rock, who trains my hands for war, and my fingers for battle. (Psalm 144:1)

A handful of verses use the word Baruch to refer to a human being, but these are exceptions rather than the rule. Nonetheless, there are enough instances of that usage so that, in the case of the prophet Baruch, we then understand this as indicating that the prophet himself is a blessed person. Baruch is a wonderful name, and other individuals have borne it. In addition to the biblical author named Baruch, there are two individuals by that name mentioned in the Book of Nehemiah (Nehemiah 3:20 and 11:5). Several years back, the Prime Minister of Israel was Ehud Barak and the President of Egypt was Hosni Mubarak, and it just happens that both of their names mean "blessed," one in Hebrew and the other in Arabic. St. Benedict, the founder of Western monasticism, had a name that meant "blessed" in Latin, translated into Hebrew, he would be called "Baruch."

The Wisdom Section (Baruch 4-5) ~ It seems fitting that Baruch, whose name is used in blessing God and in declaring beatitudes for human beings, would turn his attention to writing a great poem in praise of wisdom. The Wisdom Literature, which includes the Psalms, holds an important place in the Old Testament. King Solomon was offered one gift by God, and he chose wisdom and received all things besides. Wisdom is the ability to discern and put into play the right course of action. Kings need it for ruling, priests for praying, prophets for speaking, scribes

for writing, and people in all walks of life for the successful execution of their responsibilities, consistent with their state in life. What wisdom do parents need! And grandparents!

From Baruch 3:9 to end of Baruch 5, the Book of Baruch comprises a great paean to wisdom. The style is so different that some scholars believe this comes from a different author, but the theme is consistent, even if the style is not. First, there is a great question, the same issue that underlies the great prayer of contrition: "Why is it, O Israel, why is it that you are in the land of your enemies, that you are growing old in a foreign country?" (Baruch 3:10). Clearly this is wisdom in exile.

Here is the problem. If wisdom is the skill to do things successfully, how do we cope with failure? The answer is that there is an art to accepting defeat gracefully. Everyone admires an athlete or a politician who can lose a game or an election, but remain poised and courteous. Everyone must learn how to take the hard knocks of life, and a good loser is an inspiration to all, just as an arrogant winner degrades the sport of the body politic. We need gracious losers and humble winners in society.

So, the scribe Baruch, in exile, in failure, in disaster, seeks the wisdom to cope with his situation successfully. "Learn where there is wisdom, where there is strength, where there is understanding, that you may at the same time discern where there is length of days, and life, where there is light for the eyes, and peace" (Baruch 3:14).

Baruch asks, "Who has gone up into heaven, and taken her (wisdom), and brought her down from the clouds? Who has gone over the sea, and found her, and will buy her for pure gold?" (Baruch 3:29-30). Job, in the midst of his trials, similarly asks, "Whence then comes wisdom? And where is the place of understanding? It is hid from the eyes of all living, and concealed from the birds of the air" (Job 28:20-21).

God knows wisdom, and placed her in nature, and revealed her in his commandments. "She is the book of the commandments of God, and the law that endures forever. All who hold her fast will live, and those who forsake her will die" (Baruch 4:1). Here, Baruch, after the fall of the southern kingdom, comes to the same conclusion that the prophet Micah reached after the fall of the northern kingdom, namely, that the people would survive only by persevering in their practice of the law of God. In exile, obedience to the law of God is the only wisdom that will allow the people to survive.

Jerusalem Speaks. After Baruch praises wisdom (Baruch 3:9-4:9), now the abandoned city of Jerusalem speaks, like a mother who grieves after all her children have left the nest. "With joy I nurtured them, but I sent them away with weeping and sorrow" (Baruch 4:11). Nonetheless, there is a voice of encouragement for her faraway children: "Take courage, my children, cry to God, and he will deliver you from the power and hand of the enemy. For I have put my hope in the Everlasting to save you, and joy has come to me from the Holy One, because of the mercy which soon will come to you from your everlasting Savior. For I sent you out with sorrow and weeping, but God will give you back to me with joy and gladness for ever" (Baruch 4:21-23).

Surely these are among the inspired Sacred Scriptures. People don't just write things like this without the inspiration of the Holy Spirit. These words foreshadow the grief of the Blessed Virgin Mary for her crucified Son, the grief of the Church for her fallen-away and indifferent

children, the grief of the heavenly Jerusalem looking down upon an earth that seems determined to fall from grace—these are griefs that are full of hope, and even of joy, because of the great confidence that we have in the infinite mercy and power of God.

Baruch Speaks Again. Finally, the scribe Baruch speaks again. Just as the personified city had offered a word of encouragement to her exiled citizens, now Baruch offers encouragement to the city. "Take courage, O Jerusalem, for he who named you will comfort you" (Baruch 4:30). The name "Salem," which is contained within Jerusalem, means "Peace."

In his old age, Baruch has developed a streak of bitterness that was not present before. Now he no longer prays for long days for Nebuchadnezzar, but rather he prophesies: "Wretched will be the cities which your children served as slaves, wretched will be the city which received your sons. For just as she rejoiced at your fall and was glad for your ruin, so she will be grieved at her own desolation. And I will take away her pride in her great population, and her insolence will be turned to grief. For fire will come upon her from the Everlasting for many days, and for a long time she will be inhabited by demons" (Baruch 4:32-35).

This prophecy of doom for Babylon, combined with the vision of return for the Jewish exiles, is the closest thing to an actual prophesy in the whole Book of Baruch. He never uses the prophetic formulae such as "The Lord spoke …," or "This is the Word of the Lord." Finally, Baruch gets his chance to issue a great prophecy of his own: "Look toward the east, O Jerusalem, and see the joy that is coming to you from God! Behold, your sons are coming, whom you sent away, they are coming, gathered from east and west, at the word of the Holy One, rejoicing in the glory of God" (Baruch 4:36-37).

The final vision of Baruch resembles those of the prophet Isaiah. "For God has ordered that every high mountain and the everlasting hills be made low and the valleys filled up, to make level ground, so that Israel may walk safely in the glory of God. The woods and every fragrant tree have shaded Israel at God's command" (Baruch 5:7-8). One who walked forth into exile, who knew the agony of walking through deep valleys and the exhaustion of climbing mountain ranges and the dehydration from walking through unshaded trails describes a return from exile in entirely different terms. Israel was led chained into captivity, but shall return with a first-class ticket.

The Letter of Jeremiah ~ Some editions of the Bible are lacking a sixth chapter, but in those cases the chapter becomes a separate book under the title "The Letter of Jeremiah." This is a letter that Jeremiah dictated to Baruch and sent with him to be read to the exiles in Babylon. Jeremiah himself went into exile to the west, to Egypt. When they separated, Jeremiah stopped writing, but Baruch started writing in his own name.

The Letter of Jeremiah really belongs not at the end of the Book of Baruch, but at the end of the Book of Jeremiah. Some scholars question whether the letter is the work of Jeremiah or Baruch. It is actually an extended sermon against idolatry, and contains a warning that must have been very important at the time of the exile. The people were going to alien lands that had alien gods, but that did not mean that the people had to adopt an alien religion and forsake the one, true God.

> Since you know then that they are not gods, do not fear them.
> For they can neither curse nor bless kings;
> they cannot show signs in the heavens and among the nations,
> or shine like the sun or give light like the moon.
> The wild beasts are better than they are,
> for they can flee to cover and help themselves.
> So we have no evidence whatever that they are gods;
> therefore do not fear them.
> *Letter to Jeremiah, verses 65-69*

Surely this is an important biblical message. So many times in so many passages, the Word of God tells us, "Fear not!" Fear is a kind of false worship. If the world, the flesh and the devil cannot get us to worship them in any other way, they will attempt to frighten us into submission. The courage with which we look the world in the eye fearlessly is the freedom from false worship. Baruch and his generation had to look fearlessly into a brave new world where the Kingdom of Israel and the Kingdom of Judah were no longer on the map. By clinging to God in their hearts, they bestowed upon the world the religion of the one, true God.

> "Divine Scripture, addressing itself to those who love themselves and to the boastful, says most excellently: 'Where are the princes of the nations, and those who rule over the nations, and those who rule over the beasts which are upon the earth; they that take their diversion among the birds of the air; they that hoard up silver, and the gold in which men trust—and there is no end to their acquiring it; they that work in silver and in gold and are solicitous? There is no searching of their works; they have vanished and have gone down into Hades' (Baruch 3:16-19)."
> St. Clement of Alexandria (150-216 AD), *The Instructor of Children*, 2.3.

What can be the antidote to sin and idolatry in any age for any person?

> **"Love unites us to God;** it cancels innumerable sins, has no limit to its endurance, bears everything patiently. Love is neither servile nor arrogant. It does not provoke schisms or form cliques, but always acts in harmony with others. By it all God's chosen ones have been sanctified; without it, it is impossible to please Him. . . . Happy are we, beloved, if love enables us to live in harmony and in the observance of God's commandments, for then it will also gain for us the remission of our sins. Scripture pronounces *happy those whose transgressions are pardoned, whose sins are forgiven. Happy the man to whom the Lord imputes no fault, on whose lips there is not guile.* This is the blessing given those whom God has chosen through Jesus Christ our Lord. To Him be glory for ever and ever."
> St. Clement I of Rome, Pope (+101 AD), *Letter to the Corinthians*, 49-50.

1. How is God described in Baruch 3:1-6?

2. What happened to the people and why? Baruch 3:3-11

3. Compare the following verses.

Deuteronomy 30:19	
Psalm 16:11	
Proverbs 4:20-23	
Baruch 3:9	
John 10:10b	
John 14:6	

4. How did the people lose their peace?   Baruch 3:10-14

5. "Wisdom" is sometimes translated "prudence" (Baruch 3:9, 14). What is prudence? *CCC 1806*

6. Where could you find the wisdom spoken of in Baruch 3:15-4:4?

Deuteronomy 4:1-6	
Proverbs 9:10	
Wisdom 6:10-20	
Sirach 39:1-4	
Luke 21:14-15	

7. When you think of a contemporary people with wisdom, who comes to mind?

8. Find a cause and effect described in Baruch 4:5-20.

9. What caused the problems of the people in exile?

Baruch 1:13	
Baruch 1:19-22	
Baruch 2:5, 12	
Baruch 3:3-5	
Baruch 4:7-8	
Baruch 4:12-13	

10. Today, when people encounter adversity, who do they blame?

11. When chastisements come, what should you do?

Baruch 4:21	
Baruch 4:27	
Baruch 4:28	
Matthew 11:28-30	

12. Compare the following verses.

Isaiah 40:9-11	
Isaiah 43:5	
Baruch 4:36-37	

13. How many emotions can you identify in Baruch 5? Write them below.

14. What can you learn about God's anger from Psalm 30?

15. Compare the following verses.

Isaiah 61:10-11	
Jeremiah 33:16	
Baruch 5:1-4	

16. What is foretold in the following verses.

Isaiah 40:3-5	
Isaiah 41:19-20	
Baruch 5:7-8	

17. Can you find comfort in the verses below?

Isaiah 49:13-16	
Isaiah 49:25	
Baruch 5:9	

18. Have you ever felt exiled from God due to your own folly or sinfulness?

19. What can you do when you get into a mess? Acts 4:19 or Psalm 32:5

20. Pray the Act of Contrition that you use for Confession right now.

Monthly Social Activity

This month your small group will meet for coffee, tea, or a simple breakfast or lunch in someone's home.

Pray for this social event and for the host or hostess.

Try if at all possible to attend.

Offer hospitality for one of the socials to be held at your home.

Prophets and Apostles shared words of wisdom.

Now reflect on your own personal life.

~ What helpful word of wisdom was passed on to you?

~ When and by whom?

~ What word of wisdom could you pass on to others?

DANIEL 1-6
The Prophet in His Youth

Memory Verse

**"Blessed be the name of God forever and ever, to whom belong wisdom and might.
He changes times and season; he removes kings and sets up kings;
he gives wisdom to the wise and knowledge to those who have understanding;
he reveals deep and mysterious things;
he knows what is in the darkness and the light dwells with him."**

DANIEL 2:20-22

Meet Daniel. In the sixth verse, we receive a formal introduction to the prophet Daniel. King Nebuchadnezzar, desiring to tap the creativity of the captive people of Israel, recruits several of their young men to be educated to serve at his court. Actually, it was no doubt the practice of the king to recruit some of the young nobles from each of the component peoples of his empire, which has been standard practice in many empires down to modern times.

The Romans used to enroll the sons of their subject kings in special schools in Rome, to discourage the kings from attempting to revolt. If they did so, their sons could be killed. In effect, the scholarships for the noble youths were a form a hostage taking. King Herod the Great was loyal to Rome because he himself had studied in Rome and had grown up as a personal friend of the young Octavian, later Augustus Caesar.

In a continuation of the ancient oriental practice, the Ottoman Turks drafted promising young men from all their subject nations and took them to Istanbul to be educated and incorporated into the Sultan's court. The selection of Daniel and the other young men for court service in Babylon is not just a literary device, then, but an accurate description of historical practices. Daniel was honored but also imprisoned by the opportunity to serve the king.

Three other Hebrew youths serve along with Daniel. They are all described as belonging to the "tribe of Judah." This means one of two things: (a) that these four youths were among the last wave of exiles to reach Babylon, or (b) that they come from the nobility, even from the royal family. It can and probably does mean both of these things.

Initially the chapter mentions only the four Jewish youths, but it becomes clear by verse 13 that there are other young men of diverse nationality who also are serving in the courts of the king. They might have been Chaldean, Mede, Persian, Assyrian, Phoenician, Hittite or any number of other races that inhabited the Kingdom of Babylon, which had inherited the ethnic diversity created as a matter of policy by the Assyrian Empire before them.

The name Daniel means "God is My Judge" in Hebrew. The word for God in Hebrew is El. Do not think of the Book of Judges. That is a different word in Hebrew. Those judges were neither elected nor crowned and ruled by a special divine charism, but they were merely human, offering purely administrative justice. Divine justice is qualitatively different. God judges perfectly.

God Himself, a discerning judge, penetrates the very heart of man. God reads every thought of the heart perfectly and precisely. You cannot be "misjudged" by God. At the end of time, God will judge the earth, and not with human judgment, which is fallible and often wrong.

The name Daniel first appears in a list of the kings of Ugarit, which flourished on the Syrian coast at least twelve centuries before Christ. Apparently this king was very astute, and these accolades have survived in the Ugaritic literature about him: "He judges the cause of the widow, he tries the case of the orphan" (Tale of Aqhat, V:7-8).

The fame of King Dnil (as it was spelled) was so great that he became legendary throughout the region for his wisdom. Many centuries later, he takes his place alongside Noah and Job, two other heroes of proverbial wisdom: "[W]hen a land sins against me by acting faithlessly, and I stretch out my hand against it, and break its staff of bread and send famine upon it, and cut off from it man and beast, even if these three men, Noah, Daniel, and Job, were in it, they would deliver but their own lives by their righteousness, says the Lord GOD" (Ezekiel 14:13-14).

No doubt the parents of Daniel the prophet were aware of the legendary ruler after whom they named their son at his circumcision. Just as today we give the names of saints to our children at baptism, so the Israelites bestowed names of holy and virtuous people from the past onto their children. The boy Daniel had to live up to his name, and he succeeded beyond all expectations.

We do not know Daniel's father's name. Nowhere is he call "Daniel, son of so-and-so." This takes him out of the realm of history and puts him into a special, mysterious zone. Of course, he moves in the palaces of historical kings at great turning points in history. He himself, however, has a quality of timelessness, because he is so close to the wisdom of God.

The new name Belteshazzar, meaning "The Lord's Prince" in Akkadian, is given to Daniel by the chief eunuch of the royal court. While not an exact translation of the name Daniel from Hebrew into Akkadian, it does contains two nouns. The word *BEL* in Akkadian means "Lord" and the word *ZAR* means "Prince." Notice the word *ZAR* at the end of the king's own name— Nebuchadnezzar. Daniel's new name is very significant, because the king's son (historically, his grandson) bears a version of the same name—Belshazzar. When Daniel served the heir to the throne, Belteshezzar served Belshazzar.

Why did Daniel receive a new name? Apparently this was common practice in the court, for Daniel's three companions also receive the names by which they are traditionally known, Shadrach, Meshach and Abednego. The book tells us that the new courtiers took a three-year course of instruction during which they learned the Chaldean (Aramaic) language. However, these new names are not Chaldean or Aramaic, but Akkadian.

The New Kingdom of Babylon used Akkadian for its official records, for this was the language of administration since the time of Hammurabi during the Old Kingdom period more than a thousand years before. The rise of Babylon occurred under a Chaldean dynasty, and that was probably the actual language spoken at court. The courtiers who could read and write would have to know Akkadian, but the courtiers who were illiterate would only need to know Chaldean.

Now the Chaldeao-Aramaic language resembles Hebrew. The name Daniel makes perfect and identical sense in both languages. There would have been no need for him to get a new name if the court used only Chaldean. The forms of tradition had to be observed, however. The very legitimacy of the kingdom depended upon stressing the cultural continuity with the Old Kingdom. So everybody had Akkadian names, but they did not use them very much. Within the Book of Daniel, the prophet himself is called Daniel 48 times, but Belshazzar only 10 times. That is a ratio of nearly five to one, and it probably reflects the rate of usage of Aramaic over Akkadian in the Babylonian court.

When Cyrus the Great overthrows the Babylonian Empire, he abolishes the use of Akkadian and elevates Aramaic to the language of administration for the entire Persian Empire. From Greece to Egypt to Persia, Aramaic become the lingua franca of the largest empire the world had ever seen. Everybody had to know two languages, then: their native tongue and Aramaic. This arrangement was particularly beneficial for the Jews, because their Hebrew language was so close to Aramaic. Hebrew and Aramaic have the same alphabet, similar grammar and nearly coextensive vocabulary. Jews everywhere in the Persian Empire could flourish in business and bureaucracy, because the official language of the state was so close to their own. There were many "Daniels," who rose to high station with ease, and partly for linguistic reasons.

Daniel's Ups and Downs ~ Many similarities exist between the prophet Daniel and the patriarch Joseph. Both were precocious youths who ended up in a foreign land—Joseph was sold into slavery in Egypt, while Daniel was taken away into exile in Babylon. Both rose from adversity to a high level in their places of sojourn—Joseph became steward for Potiphar, while Daniel was recruited as a page at the court of Babylon. Both experience a fall from their new heights—Joseph is falsely accused by Potiphar's wife and cast into prison, while Daniel risks being executed with all the magicians of the kingdom. Both overcome their new trials to rise even higher, both become royal counselors, and both provide critical advice during major events in national history—the drought in Egypt, and the impending military collapse of Babylon.

In its overall genre, the Book of Daniel reads more like a historical narrative than a prophetic text. Prophetic books contain many oracles from the Lord, but Daniel has few of these. Instead, like the little Book of Jonah, this is really a biography of the prophet himself. The prophet's own life contains the meaning, and the virtues of the prophet are meant to be an example to us. Jews read the Book of Daniel and see in his life a pattern for the whole people and their conduct in their affairs while exiled throughout the world; Christians read the Book of Daniel and find an inspiration for their personal lives in their sojourn as foreigners in this universe.

In narratives such as these, the ups and downs constitute an important theological message. Both prosperity and adversity contain hidden dangers. In prosperity, we tend to forget God and believe that good things have come to us because of our own merits rather than because of His goodness. In adversity, we tend to blame God and believe that we have been deprived of health or happiness because of the withdrawal of His favor. We have been placed upon earth in order to prove our worth before God, and we need the ups and downs of life in order to demonstrate to ourselves and to Him what kind of mettle we have. The great personalities of the Bible have many changes of fortune, but what they all have in common is fidelity and perseverance. *They were God's friends in good times, and also in bad ones. Any other kind is not really friendship at all.*

The Trial of the Young Daniel ~ We meet Daniel at the beginning of the book when he is a young man, and he confronts his first crisis as a youth. Hence we tend to think of Daniel that way, even though he lived seventy years more to see the fall of Babylon.

The first half of the Book of Daniel covers the several crises that Daniel had to face in the court of Kings Nebuchadnezzar and Belshazzar of Babylon:

- Daniel refuses to eat non-kosher food and thrives on a vegetarian diet (Chapter 1).
- He interprets two royal dreams (Chapters 2 and 4).
- Daniel and his three friends refuse to worship a gold idol, and he sees them thrown into a fiery furnace (Chapter 3).
- He interprets the handwriting on the wall (Chapter 5).

Each of these episodes represents a threat to Daniel and to the exiled Jewish people, who must demonstrate their continuing survival skills. Each episode vividly treats some important biblical issue—fidelity to Mosaic law, idolatry, prophecy or wisdom. The most significant is the chapter 2 dream.

King Nebuchadnezzar and Daniel have the same dream, which only Daniel can retell and interpret. The statue made of several different materials represents a vision of history: "The head of this image was of fine gold, its breast and arms of silver, its belly and thighs of bronze, its legs of iron, its feet partly or iron and partly of clay" (Daniel 2:32). These seem to be the successive empires that ruled the Near East during the First Millennium before Christ. From the seventh to the second centuries the Empires of Assyria, Babylonia, Persia, the Hellenistic Kingdoms and Rome succeeded each other. Five empires ruled in five hundred years. They overlapped each other in their rising and falling, but still each of them knew only about a hundred years of true hegemony. The result was unsettling for the peoples of the region, such as the Jews, who lacked the conditions of historical stability in which to pursue their lives.

The very matter of language was confusing, since some of these empires brought different official tongues into administration. In the East, the Romans used Greek rather than Latin, and the Babylonians retained the Assyrian administrative system. Even so there were three different languages of administration in half a millennium—Akkadian, Aramaic and Greek. Interestingly, the Book of Daniel itself reflects this confusion of tongues. The beginning of the book is written in Hebrew, the middle in Aramaic and the end in Hebrew again. Over and above that, there are three Greek chapters (Chapter 3 in part, and Chapters 13 and 14), which are excluded from the Protestant canon of Scripture.

Scholars have debated over which language was original to the Book of Daniel. The best explanation is that the whole text was composed in Aramaic, and that the beginning and ending were later translated into Hebrew, so that the book could be included in the "Hebrew Bible." Thank goodness at least part of the book was left in Aramaic, because it is one of the few texts that allow us to see the language used by Jews before the coming of Jesus, who spoke this as His mother tongue.

The Canticle of the Three Young Men (sometimes misleadingly called the Canticle of Daniel) appears in Daniel chapter 3 in Greek. Scholars today believe that this canticle, though surviving only in Greek translation, was originally composed in Hebrew or Aramaic, even before the rest of the Book of Daniel. Remember how there is a Psalm contained in the middle of the Book of Jonah? Remember how the Book of Joel, near its midpoint, quotes the beginning of another Psalm? There seems to be a pattern at work, with a Canticle to be found in the middle of some of the prophetic books. The presence of the Canticle of the Three Youths makes sense in Daniel 3. As a matter of fact, there does seem to be something missing after verse 23 when the Canticle is omitted.

The Canticle, prayed in part every Sunday during Morning Prayer in the Divine Office, is one of the most beautiful pieces of writing in the entire Bible, and its omission would be a severe impoverishment. Clearly the Canticle comes from the same universe of thought, perhaps even from the same human author, as the creation account in the first chapter of Genesis:

(1) "And God said, 'Let there be light'" (Genesis 1:3)
~ The Canticle responds: "Blessed art thou in the temple of thy holy glory and to be extolled and highly glorified for ever" (Daniel 3:31 RSV, [53 NAB]).

(2) "And God said, 'Let there be a firmament'" (Genesis 1:6)
~ The Canticle replies: "Blessed art thou in the firmament of heaven and to be sung and glorified for ever" (Daniel 3:34 RSV, [56 NAB]).

(3) "And God said, 'Let the waters under the heavens be gathered'" (Genesis 1:9)
~ The Canticle answers: "Bless the Lord, seas and rivers, sing praise to him and highly exalt him for ever" (Daniel 3:56 RSV, [78 NAB]).

(4) "And God said, 'Let there be lights in the firmament'" (Genesis 1:14)
~ The Canticle adds: "Bless the Lord, sun and moon, sing praise to him and highly exalt him for ever" (Daniel 3:40 RSV, [62 NAB]).

(5) "And God said, 'Let the waters bring forth swarms of living creatures'" (Genesis 1:20)
~ The Canticle counters: "Bless the Lord, you whales and all creatures that move in the waters, sing praise to him and highly exalt him for ever" (Daniel 3:57 RSV, [79 NAB]).

(6) "Then God said, 'Let us make man in our image'" (Genesis 1:26)
~ The Canticle continues: ""Bless the Lord, you sons of men, sing praise to him and highly exalt him for ever" (Daniel 3:60 RSV, [82 NAB]).

****Depending on which Bible translation you have, you may have to hunt around in your Bible and search for the Canticle and the numbering of these verses may be different.***

1. Read Daniel 1-6 and write your favorite verse. *Note that different Bibles will have different formatting and different placement of chapters and verses. Don't be frustrated. Persevere!*

2. List the names of the young men of Judah and their new names. Daniel 1:6-7

Daniel	*Belteshazzar*

3. Describe some of the characteristics of these young men. Daniel 1:3-7, 17, 20

Daniel 1:3-7	
Daniel 1:17	
Daniel 1:20	

4. In your own words, describe the drama in Daniel 1:8-21.

5. Describe the king's problem and his edict from Daniel 2:1-13.

6. Chronicle Daniel's behavior in the midst of this crisis.   Daniel 2:14-26.

Daniel 2:14-15	
Daniel 2:16	
Daniel 2:17-18	
Daniel 2:19-23	
Daniel 2:24	

7. How can the mysteries of life be solved?   Daniel 2:28

8. What does God promise in the following verses?

Daniel 2:44-45	
Luke 20:17-18	

9. What happened to the king, Daniel, Shadrach, Meshach and Abednego? Daniel 2:47-49

10. Describe the situation in Daniel 3:1-12.

11. How did Nebuchadnezzar respond to the report of the Chaldeans?   Daniel 3:13-15.

12. What response did Shadrach, Meshach, and Abednego give the king?   Daniel 3:16-18

13. Who accompanied the three young men into the furnace? Daniel 3:26 RSV, Daniel 3:49 NAB

14. From the "Canticle of the Three Young Men," write two verses of intercession.

15. From the "Canticle of the Three Young Men," write two verses of praise to God.

16. Find a verse of thanksgiving from the "Canticle of the Three Young Men." Give the verse.

17. Find as many parallel verses between Psalm 148 and the Canticle in Daniel 3 as you can.

Psalm 148	*Daniel 3*

18. Explain the dream in Daniel 4:1-14.

19. To whom did the king go for interpretation and why? Daniel 4:18 RSV, Daniel 4:15 NAB,

20. How did Daniel interpret the dream?   Daniel 4:16-27

21. What ultimately happened to King Nebuchadnezzar? Daniel 4:27-37.

22. Describe the drama in Daniel 5.

23. What is the meaning of MENE, TEKEL and PERES?   Daniel 5:25-28.

MENE	
TEKEL	
PERES	

24. What happened to Daniel in Daniel 6, and who set him up?   Daniel 6:1-18

25. How was this situation resolved?   Daniel 6:19-29

26. What did King Darius learn about God?   Daniel 6:27-28

27. What was the result for Daniel? Daniel 6:28 [29 NAB]

DANIEL 7-14
Daniel in Old Age

Memory Verse

**"I saw in the night visions, and behold with the clouds of heaven
there came one like a son of man,
and he came to the Ancient of Days,
and was presented before him.
And to him was given dominion and glory and kingdom,
that all people, nations, and languages should serve him;
his dominion is an everlasting dominion, which shall not pass away,
and his kingdom one that shall not be destroyed."**

DANIEL 7:13-14

Daniel in Old Age ~ The first half of the Book of Daniel describes the prophet as a very young man, a teenager in training as a page and then as a counselor in the court of King Nebuchadnezzar of Babylon. More than seventy years intervene, and then Daniel reappears as an administrator and counselor for King Darius I of Persia. Daniel must be no more than 15 years old in the first chapters of the book but more than 85 years old in the final chapters. The ministry of Daniel across a lifetime fulfills the prophecy, "Your sons and daughters shall prophesy, your old men shall dream dreams, and your young men shall see visions" (Joel 2:28).

The first half of the book makes easier reading, for it appears in a coherent narrative style. Each youthful episode is self-contained, presenting a distinct moral point. The second half of the book is a bit disjointed, as if written in haste or without the same measure of reflection. Someone seems to have written the first half of the book while Daniel was still alive to recount the events of his youth, while the events of old age may have been described only after Daniel himself was no longer available to clarify certain points. There may have been two or more different authors for the different parts of this book, authors of differing narratorial skill.

The editor of the second half of Daniel does not seem to observe the classical unities of time and place. The chapters do not appear in a strict chronological sequence. Chapter 6 takes place under Darius of Persia, but chapters 7 and 8 revert to the Babylonian era, and then chapters 9 and following return to the Persian epoch. This may constitute an early version of a "flash-back," a typical cinematic device, but it could also result from poor editing.

Cyrus and the rulers of Persian after him bore the title "Shah of Shahs," which means "King of Kings." Eventually this would come to be applied to Jesus Christ. Theologically, God is Ruler of the rulers of the earth. In the original, political sense, the Persian Emperor was the master of all the potentates who were subject to him. Although addressing the king of Babylon, the Book of Daniel uses this political title once: "You, O king (are) the king of kings, to whom the God of heaven has given the kingdom, the power, and the might, and the glory" (Daniel 2:37).

Interestingly, the Book of Daniel soon afterward coins a divine appellative, "God of gods," that is clearly copied from the political one: "Truly your God is the God of gods and Lord of kings and a revealer of mysteries" (Daniel 2:47). Although these verses occur in the first half of the book in connection with the Kingdom of Babylon, the terminology they use is actually Persian and would fit more precisely in the second part of the book.

One should also note that the first Persian emperor was not Darius but Cyrus the Great. Chapters 6 and 9 take place under Darius, and then chapters 10-12 under Cyrus, referring back to Darius as if in the past. One can hardly believe that the author of Daniel did not know that Cyrus had founded the Persian Empire, for it was he who allowed the Jews to return and begin rebuilding the temple. The Jews received Cyrus as an agent of God Almighty, and placed him on a high, nearly messianic pedestal.

We cannot assume that the author of Daniel was ignorant of this turning point of Jewish history. There were three men named Darius who ruled the Persian Empire, but all three came after Cyrus the Great. Therefore we must conclude that historical chronology was irrelevant to the author's purpose in writing the second half of the book. Here the narrative proceeds not chronologically but through association of ideas. The theological sense is more important than the historical in this part of the book. *The first half of Daniel is biographical, the second half is mystical.*

Daniel and Jeremiah ~ At the beginning of chapter 9, Daniel finds a text in the Book of Jeremiah: "This whole land shall become a ruin and a waste, and these nations shall serve the king of Babylon seventy years. Then after seventy years are completed, I will punish the king of Babylon and that nation, the land of the Chaldeans, for their iniquity, says the LORD, making their land an everlasting waste" (Jeremiah 25:11-12).

Reading farther in the same book, Daniel finds the verse: "For thus says the LORD: When seventy years are completed for Babylon, I will visit you, and I will fulfil to you my promise and bring you back to this place" (Jeremiah 29:10).

Daniel meditates deeply on these truly prophetic passages, and prays a lengthy prayer (Daniel 9:4-19), which is reminiscent of the letters of Baruch and Jeremiah, which we have already studied. What is of greatest interest at this point is how the prophet Daniel accepts the Book of Jeremiah as part of Sacred Scripture. We see one prophet dependent upon the insights of a previous prophet.

Now the Book of Jeremiah refers back to his predecessor Micah as a true prophet (Jeremiah 26:18), and this reference is found in the same part of the book as Jeremiah's reference to the seventy years. Therefore, it is clear that Daniel accepted both Jeremiah and Micah as his true prophetic predecessors. A line of authentic prophecy had by then become clear, leading from Micah (the contemporary of Isaiah) to Jeremiah to Daniel.

Remember that at this time, much of the Old Testament had not even been written, and the Bible did not yet exist in a single collection. Different books were then circulating as individual scrolls, and readers might have known only some of the books that were already available. We are blessed to know that Daniel accepted Jeremiah, but it is not really surprising. After all, Jeremiah's scribe Baruch had gone into captivity in Babylon, and no doubt had taken

a final edition of the Book of Jeremiah into exile with him. Since Jeremiah had prophesied the victory of Babylon over Egypt, and the seventy-year exile in Babylon, that book would have been very important reading for the exiles such as Daniel. If Daniel was 15 years old at the time he was taken into captivity in Babylon, he could even have known the prophet Jeremiah personally, as well as his scribe Baruch. The Kingdom of Judah was a tiny state with a small ruling elite, and a prophet as notorious as Jeremiah would certainly have captured everyone's notice, including the young nobles like Daniel.

So Daniel in his old age read the book of the prophet who had flourished at the time of his childhood, and he meditates on the fulfillment of biblical prophecy even as it continues to unfold in his own mystical experience.

Daniel and the Archangel Gabriel ~ Daniel, during the long course of his life, had the opportunity to meet many kings. He probably knew the last King of Judah in his childhood. He knew Kings Nebuchadnezzar and Belshazzar of Babylon, and Kings Cyrus and Darius I of Persia. While functioning as counselor to the former and administrator for the latter, he no doubt met many visiting dignitaries, including ambassadors, kings and potentates coming on state visits and to present tribute. The Persian royal capital of Persepolis is decorated with scenes of tributaries from many different "peoples, nations and languages" (Daniel 3:4, 29) bringing annual taxes to present to the emperor.

The most important personage whom Daniel ever had the privilege to meet, however, was the Archangel Gabriel, who comes to him three times. In chapter 8, Gabriel interprets for Daniel his dream of the two-horned ram. In chapter 9, the archangel interprets for Daniel the expression "seventy" from the Book of Jeremiah. After Daniel's vision by the riverside in chapter 10, Gabriel returns a third time and dictates nearly three full chapters. The second half of the Book of Daniel could be practically called the Book of Gabriel.

There is a real tenderness of feeling between this human being and the archangel. Gabriel calls the prophet "Beloved" (Daniel 10:11). Daniel, for his part, seems to be terrified by the majesty of his visitor, for in the same verse, Daniel trembles. Gabriel must repeatedly comfort him by saying, "Fear not" (Daniel 10:12) and, "O man greatly beloved, fear not" (Daniel 10:19).

This is the same archangel who will appear to Zachary and Mary in the Gospel of Luke, to announce the birth of John the Baptist and of Jesus. To both of them he says, "Do not be afraid," just as he had said to Daniel. Gabriel seems to be some kind of an intimidating presence, so he has to reassure everyone to whom he appears. Certainly the Annunciation of Christ's Incarnation was Gabriel's finest hour, the greatest task that any angelic being ever had to perform, even greater than Michael's battle with Satan. We meet Gabriel for the first time, however, here in Daniel.

In Luke, Gabriel is an archangel of few words. He says only seven verses to Zachary (Luke 1:13-17, 19-21) and only eight verses to Mary (Luke 1:28, 30-33, 35-37). By contrast, he is positively verbose here in Daniel. He does not let Daniel get a word in edgewise for the better part of five chapters. Frankly, his expositions are not crystal-clear, and only seem to make the mysteries even more mysterious. His are the kind of explanations that a rocket scientist might give to the simple question, "Why do satellites orbit the earth?"

Chapter 11 is particularly notable as a lengthy, coded essay on world history. If you know the history already, the explanation makes sense, but otherwise there will hardly be any meaning to it at all. This is early apocalyptic, a style of writing that will eventually find its ultimate expression in the Book of Revelation. Anybody can write apocalyptically by substituting general terms for specific ones. For example, Gabriel refers to the Ptolemaic ruler of Egypt as "the king of the south" and to the Seleucid ruler of Syria as "the king of the north." The resulting discourse is enigmatic, but not particularly enlightening.

We could write a modern history of Western Europe by calling Germany the "ruler of the east" and France the "ruler of the west." Then a century of conflict between these two powers could be summarized in Gabriel-like language: "the ruler of the west declared war on the ruler of the east to prevent him from unifying his kingdom. The ruler of the east invaded the west and took Strasbourg. Several decades later, the two rulers fought again, and this time the ruler of the west took back Strasbourg. Several decades later, the ruler of the east took over the entire kingdom of the west, but was completely defeated a few years later and had to cede Strasbourg back again. Eventually, Strasbourg became the parliamentary capital of Europe, with representatives from both rulers meeting together there."

Apocalyptic discourse, instead of clarifying things, seems to emphasize the confusion. The reader feels relieved to be viewing a chaotic situation from a certain safe vantage point. No matter how confused we may be, it could be worse. We could live in Strasbourg, where everyone has French first names and German last names, and speaks German at home but French in public!

Although Daniel's vision is encrypted history, the ultimate message is eternal, and takes place after the end of history. The final kingship is not Rome, as a purely historical analysis would indicate, but Heaven. The ultimate moral of all apocalyptic writing is Jesus' forthright remark to Pilate, "My kingship is not of this world" (John 18:36).

Daniel and the Lions ~ Daniel finds himself thrust into the lions' den not once, but twice, in the longer form of the book. The first time (chapter 6) he is being punished for offering prayers facing toward Jerusalem after the king had forbidden any prayers to any gods in the whole kingdom for thirty days, except to the king himself. This was a kind of state atheism, like that practiced in the Communist world, where any and every religion was equally anathematized. The second time (chapter 14) Daniel is being punished for slaying Bel the Dragon. This time the lions have been given a daily diet of two human beings to get ready for eating Daniel, and he is left with them for seven days to be sure of their eating him. The lions starve rather than eat Daniel, and he himself receives a miraculous gift of food.

In both cases, the king sympathizes with Daniel but is powerless to save him from the imperfect workings of the Persian justice system. Though Daniel had already given extraordinary service to the government, when he became an embarrassment to those in power, they were only too ready to throw him into the lions' den. Down through history the powerful have known how to use people and how to discard them. Absolute monarchs used to hire and fire ministers with proverbial ease. Now, in democratic countries, the voters exercise their right to throw elected officials out of office whenever they no longer seem useful to them, straight from the heights of power into oblivion.

The kings of Assyria kept lions for sport, as noted earlier. For the Babylonians, the lion was a symbol of Ishtar, goddess of love and war. The Temple of Ishtar was one of the most impressive buildings of the city. Today the processional way and Ishtar Gate from Babylon have been reconstructed in the Pergamon Museum in Berlin. One can also visit the foundations of the Ishtar Temple on the original site of Babylon south of Baghdad.

No historical evidence from this period indicates that the Babylonians or Persians ever fed people to the lions. Certainly there is plenty of evidence from a later period. The Romans threw many Christians to the lions. Of so many, one thinks particularly of the martyr Felicity, who was cast into the arena, along with her friend Perpetua.

Because the lion is not only a real animal but also a symbol for the goddess Ishtar, Daniel's survival during his two sojourns with the lions has a theological significance. The animals that represent the false god treat respectfully the prophet of the true God. This shows the power of the One God over all others. This underlying message of the lion episodes clearly coincides with the point of the episodes against idolatry, when Daniel insists on praying to his own God despite the king's ordinance, and when he destroys the idol, Bel.

The suspension of the natural law of "eat or be eaten" inside the lions' den is itself the fruit of prophecy. Isaiah had foretold, "The wolf shall dwell with the lamb, and the leopard shall lie down with the kid, and the calf and the lion and the fatling together, and a little child shall lead them. The cow and the bear shall feed, their young shall lie down together; and the lion shall eat straw like the ox" (Isaiah 11:6-7). The great eschatological vision of Isaiah is already partially fulfilled inside the lions' den. Like Isaac in the Book of Genesis, Daniel is a sacrificial lamb that was offered to God, but at the last minute God did not require his life. The Jewish people have more reason to identify with Isaac's rescue, because they were physically spared extermination inside him, but Daniel points forward to the great final rescue at the final end times in which they also participate. They identify with Isaac through memory, with Daniel through hope. *Christians see in both of these figures foreshadowings of Christ, who is sacrificed but through resurrection overcomes the pit of death.*

Daniel and Susanna ~ Daniel was an old man during both of his visits to the lions, which took place under the Persian king Darius. Chapter 13 reverts to Daniel's youth again, which we only learn when he appears at the end of the story: "God aroused the holy spirit of a young lad named Daniel" (Daniel 13:45). It is clear that this episode relates only tangentially to the rest of the book. The Book of Daniel is like an anthology of short stories, rather than a seamless narrative.

The Jewish community in exile continue to practice Mosaic law, even though they are living under Babylonian and then Persian rule. The great empires of the Near East allowed the subject peoples to function according to their own by-laws for the most part. Sporadic attempts were made, as by the Seleucids in Syria, to customize the practices of the population, but generally each community followed its own customs regarding matrimony, worship and even criminal justice.

So, in the Susanna story, the Mosaic requirement of having two witnesses in any capital case applies. The wisdom of this arrangement becomes apparent when Daniel interrogates the witnesses separately to see if their testimony agrees. When it does not, their accusation is proven to be false. The Law of Moses is superior to modern criminal law in this regard. There are people on death row who have been condemned by purely circumstantial evidence, and DNA testing has shown that a large number of those so condemned have been innocent. If Mosaic Law had been followed, none of these innocent people would have been sent to death row. It is not fair to use the Old Testament as a precedent for capital punishment without making clear the safeguards that were built into the criminal process to protect against false accusation.

In the Old Testament we already find admirable witnesses of fidelity to the holy law of God even to the point of a voluntary acceptance of death. A prime example is the story of Susanna: in reply to the two unjust judges who threatened to have her condemned to death if she refused to yield to their sinful passion, she says: "I am hemmed in on every side. For if I do this thing, it is death for me; and if I do not, I shall not escape your hands. I choose not to do it and to fall into your hands, rather than to sin in the sight of the Lord!" (Daniel 13:22-23). Susanna, preferring to "fall innocent" into the hands of the judges, bears witness not only to her faith and trust in God but also to her obedience to the truth and to the absoluteness of the moral order. By her readiness to die a martyr, she proclaims that it is not right to do what God's law qualifies as evil in order to draw some good from it. Susanna chose for herself the "better part": hers was a perfectly clear witness, without any compromise, to the truth about the good and to the God of Israel. By her acts, she revealed the holiness of God.

Pope John Paul II, *Veritatis Splendor,* (August 6, 1993). no. 91.1.

Daniel and the Dragon ~ "There was a great dragon which the Babylonians worshipped" (Daniel 14:23). Is there any corroboration in the history of religion or archaeology for this statement?

The lion was the symbol for the Babylonian goddess Ishtar. Similarly, the god Marduk was symbolized by a griffin, a dragon-like creature with a long neck. Just as the Assyrians collected lions and confined them in a royal zoo, so the Romans collected exotic animals from Africa, to use in their gladiatorial combats and other spectacles. Animals were sacrificed throughout the Middle East, and the Jews themselves imposed the sins of the nation upon the annual "scapegoat."

The Babylonians could very easily have imported giraffes or other strange creatures and used them as living symbols for their gods. After Daniel poisons such a sacred animal (the dragon), he is thrown into a den with other such sacred animals (the lions). Clearly these stories are not just included for their biographical interest, but for theological significance. The God of Daniel is more powerful than the gods represented by griffins or lions.

 *Daniel may be a man without a country, but he is not a man without a God!* 

1. Describe the Vision of the Four Beasts from Daniel 7.

2. Compare the following verses.

Daniel 7:9-10	
Revelation 5:11	

3. Compare these passages.

Daniel 7:13	
Matthew 9:6	
Mark 2:28	
Luke 9:22	
John 1:51	
Revelation 1:13	
Revelation 14:14	

4. What is the fulfillment of Daniel's vision concerning the Son of Man? *CCC 664*

Being seated at the Father's right hand signifies ________________________________

____

____

____

____

____

____   *CCC 664*

5. Describe the vision in Daniel 8 and Daniel's response to it.   Daniel 8:27

6. Explain Daniel's words and behavior in these following passages.

Daniel 9:3	
Daniel 9:4-6	
Daniel 9:7,9	
Daniel 9:17	
Daniel 9:18-19	

7. What does Archangel Gabriel say to Daniel in Daniel 10:11-12?

8. Who is introduced in Daniel 10:13, 21?

9. What is foretold in Daniel 11?

10. Compare the following passages.

Daniel 12:1-3	
Matthew 25:45-46	
John 5:27-29	
Wisdom 3:1-8	

11. Read the story of Susanna in your Bible. Daniel 13

Who accused her?	
Who rescued her?	
How?	

12. What logic does Susanna use in making her decision when trapped?   Verse 23

13. What hope did Susanna hold onto in choosing to trust God rather than sin? *CCC 992*

14. Have you ever felt like you were trapped between two terrible choices?

15. Describe the outcome from Daniel 13:60-64.

16. Tell the story of Bel and the Dragon in your own words.   Daniel 14

17. What happened to Daniel in verses 31-32?

18. Who brought Daniel some dinner? How did he travel? Daniel 14:33-36

19. Who rescued Daniel? Daniel 14:39-42

20. What sin is described in the portrayal of Bel the Dragon? *CCC 2112*

21. List some contemporary temptations to this sin. *CCC 2113*

22. How can a person become integrated? *CCC 2114*

Human life finds ____

____________________________________. The commandment to ________________

____

________________________. Idolatry is ____

____

____

____

____. *CCC 2114*

Jude
Concerning Angels

**"But you, beloved, build yourselves up on your most holy faith;
pray in the Holy Spirit;
keep yourselves in the love of God;
wait for the mercy of our Lord Jesus Christ unto eternal life."**

JUDE 20-21

Jude's Identity ~ The writer of this little letter introduces himself in the opening verse: "Jude, a servant of Jesus Christ and brother of James" (Jude 1). This formula is very similar to the opening of the Letter of James: "James, a servant of God and of the Lord Jesus Christ" (James 1:1). Both authors refer to themselves as servants of Jesus Christ. Jude's reference to James seems to indicate that this author is familiar with the other letter.

Neither James nor Jude uses the term "apostle" or "brother of the Lord" to identify himself. Tradition has identified the author of this letter as Jude the Apostle, and later commentators have speculated that this might be Jude "the brother of the Lord." There is no proof from within the letter itself which of these two possibilities might be correct.

We should note that the name "Jude" was very popular among Jews of all ages. One of the twelve sons of Jacob was called "Judah." He received a wide swath of inheritance in the southern part of the Holy Land, which came to be known as the "Kingdom of Judah" and later "Judea." The word "Jew" itself came from the adjective "Judean" and thus the name of the religion of Judaism derives from the name "Judah."

Men of any tribe could be called "Jude," but this name would have been most popular among families of the tribe of Judah. When we encounter someone with the name Jude, we can be entitled to assume that the bearer would most likely have belonged to that tribe. In a similar way, we would assume that someone named "Stan" or "Stosh" might have Polish ancestry or a "Greta" or "Ingrid" might be of Sandinavian descent.

Among the twelve apostles, there are two who bear the name Jude:

– **Judas Iscariot** (which literally means, "Jude, the man from the town of Qaryot")
– **Jude Thaddeus** (which means, **"Jude, the man of heart"**).

Luke calls the eleventh apostle "Jude" (Luke 6:16) while St. Matthew and St. Mark in their gospel writings call the eleventh apostle "Thaddeus" (Matthew 10:3; Mark 3:18).

The New Testament mentions a "Jude, the brother of the Lord" (Matthew 13:55) and a "Jude the son of James" (Luke 6:16), and it is not certain whether these are the same person as Jude Thaddeus. Judah was a very popular name among Jews, as was James, and the biblical text does not provide us with enough information to make an exact identification. Hence, we cannot know whether the author of this letter is Jude the Apostle, or Jude the kinsman of the Lord or some other Jude, of which there were many.

The author of this letter speaks about the apostles in the third person: "But you must remember, beloved, the predictions of the apostles of our Lord Jesus Christ; they said to you, 'In the last time there will be scoffers, following their own ungodly passions'" (Jude 17-18). Now, if this were Jude the Apostle himself writing, he would have been entitled to use the first person singular "I" (as St. Peter does in his letters) or first person plural "we" (as John does in his letters). The use of the third person here seems to put the author himself at a distance from the circle of the twelve apostles, or at least shows his preference to identify with the whole body of believers.

Jude	*Peter*	*John*

Jude, a servant of Jesus Christ and brother of James   Jude 1
 	
… remember, beloved, the predictions of the apostles of our Lord Jesus Christ; they said to you
        Jude 17-18
	Peter, an apostle of Jesus Christ 1 Peter 1:1
	
	Simon Peter, a servant and apostle of Jesus Christ
	        2 Peter 1:1
	
	Beloved, I beseech you
	        1 Peter 2:11
		That which was from the beginning, which we have heard, which we have seen with our eyes, which we have looked upon and touched with our hands, concerning the word of life … we proclaim also to you
		        1 John 1:1-3

The phrase "brother of James" in verse 1 is not as helpful as it might initially seem in identifying the author. The names James and Jude were then as common as "Tom, Dick and Harry" in our own time. We would love to know more about the author Jude, but his letter contains only 23 verses and simply does not supply enough information for a certain identification.

Whoever the historical author named Jude might have been, he has bequeathed to us only 462 words of writing. Contrast this with St. Luke, who contributed 37,778 words, the largest body of literature in the New Testament. One thing both authors have in common is the ability to use third party materials in an effective manner. Both write in excellent Greek and both have "done their homework" having at their fingertips references to the Old Testament and other sources.

This letter could have been written by an elderly gentleman thinking about his impending death and wanting to leave this letter behind as his legacy. Most scholars believe his letter was written around the year 90 AD because it is quoted by 2 Peter which may have been written around the year 100 AD, which would have made this author about 20 years old at the time of the death of Jesus, which would have made him the appropriate age to be in the apostolic circle.

St. Jude

"Although no one knows how St. Jude came to be associated with impossible cases, we do have a record of how devotion to him grew in the United States. The Claretian Fathers staffed Our Lady of Guadalupe parish on the south side of Chicago in a neighborhood surrounded by steel mills. The Depression of 1929 hit the steelworkers especially hard; many lost their jobs and had no way to support their families. To counteract his parishioners' desperation and despair, Father James Tort started a novena to St. Jude. The devotion was repeated week after week throughout the Depression, then through World War II, and again through the war in Vietnam. With each new crisis St. Jude's popularity increased, and in time Our Lady of Guadalupe Church was named the National Shrine of St. Jude. Today the shrine receives hundred of thousands of petitions every year, and the Claretians publish *The Voice of St. Jude*, a newsletter that reports uplifting stories of answers to prayer."

Thomas J. Craughwell, *Saints for Every Occasion*
(Charlotte, NC: Stampley, 2001), 354.

Jude's Teaching On Angels ~ By preserving this letter as part of the canon of the New Testament, the early Church saw the human author as inspired by the Divine Author. More important than the identity of the historical author Jude is the fact that the Holy Spirit is the ultimate author.

Short though the letter may be, it contains several important teachings, especially with respect to the role of angels. Through this letter, the Holy Spirit confirms our belief in angels cautioning us that there are good angels and bad ones. A quotation from the non-biblical book of Enoch refers to the angelic host: "Behold the Lord came with his holy myriads" (verse 14). Jude speaks of both the devil and the Archangel Michael (Jude 9). The term "archangel" appears only twice in the entire Bible, once here and again in St. Paul's first letter to the Thessalonians: "For the Lord himself will descend from heaven with a cry of command, with the archangel's call, and with the sound of the trumpet of God. And the dead in Christ will rise first" (1 Thessalonians 4:16).

Michael appears in three books of the bible—Daniel, Jude and Revelation—but only Jude calls him "archangel." Hence we are indebted to Jude alone for the knowledge of Michael's status among the heavenly host. We owe a great debt of gratitude to Jude, who while leaving his own identity ambiguous, nevertheless clarifies for us the identity of the great archangel. Jude's virtue of humility is reminiscent of John the Baptist who says of Jesus, "He must increase, but I must decrease" (John 3:30).

Revelation 12:7 suggests that in the rebellion of the angels in heaven, when the bad angels fell away from their allegiance to God, St. Michael drove Satan and his legions from heaven and plunged them into the depths of Hell. St. Gabriel the Archangel speaks to the prophet Daniel calling Michael "your prince" (Daniel 10:21). St. Thomas Aquinas says, "Michael is the breath of the Redeemer's spirit, who at the End of the World will combat and destroy Antichrist as he did Lucifer in the beginning." He is invoked in sickness and at the hour of death. Traditionally, the priest and people after Mass pray to St. Michael the Archangel, beseeching his help in protecting the Church.

Prayer to St. Michael the Archangel

Saint Michael the Archangel,

defend us in battle.

Be our safeguard against the wickedness

and snares of the devil.

Restrain him, O God, we humbly pray,

and do thou, O Prince of the Heavenly Host,

by the power of God,

cast into Hell Satan and all the evil spirits,

who prowl about the world

seeking the ruin and destruction of souls.

Amen.

Despite Jude's great humility and the brevity of his letter, Jude occasionally shows great sparks of creativity. He has some highly original images not found elsewhere in the New Testament, as in his fourfold comparison of the rebellious in verses 12 and 13:
— "waterless clouds, carried along by winds"
— "fruitless trees in late autumn, twice dead, uprooted"
— "wild waves of the sea, casting up the foam of their own shame"
— "wandering stars for whom the nether gloom of darkness has been reserved forever."

Jude's Readers ~ Some of the New Testament letters are addressed to specific churches and some are not. The letter of Jude is sent like a circular letter "to those who are called, beloved in God the Father and kept for Jesus Christ" (Jude 1). This broad address encompasses more people than the address of the Letter of James: "To the twelve tribes in the Dispersion" (James 1:1).

As little as we know about the historical author of this letter, we know even less about its original readers. Just as the letter has a Spiritual Author, it also has a spiritual audience—namely ourselves. Every piece of writing in the New Testament has both an explicit and implicit author, and an explicit and implicit audience. The Holy Spirit is the Implicit Author, and we are the implicit audience. The human author may have intended to convey certain meanings to his original audience in a particular place and time, but the Divine Author intended to convey even more meaning to His ultimate audience, the spiritual readers and seekers of all time to come.

The historical sense and the spiritual sense cannot contradict each other. The human author worked in tandem with the Spiritual Author, and there is a continuity of faith and tradition linking the original readers and us. The magisterium of the church has confirmed that both senses are important to our understanding and knowledge of Scripture.

In his great encyclical "Divino afflante Spiritu," Pope Pius XII encourages an appreciation of the historical sense—we should try to appreciate what the historical author was saying to his original readers. A few years later, the great Second Vatican Council document, Dogmatic Constitution on Divine Revelation, *Dei Verbum*, decreed that we should read Holy Scripture according to the "spiritual sense"— as God is trying to speak to us as well in the inspired texts.

Jude offers his readers an excellent trinitarian formula worth memorizing: "But you, beloved, build yourselves up on your most holy faith; pray in the Holy Spirit; keep yourselves in the love of God; wait for the mercy of our Lord Jesus Christ unto eternal life" (Jude 20-21). This sentence rises to the heights of theological insight, worthy of any of the letters of St. Paul, who concludes his Second Letter to the Corinthians with a Trinitarian blessing: "The grace of the Lord Jesus Christ and the love of God and the fellowship of the Holy Spirit be with you all" (2 Corinthians 13:14).

Finally, Jude concludes his letter with a beautiful doxology. "Now to him who is able to keep you from falling and to present you without blemish before the presence of his glory with rejoicing, to the only God, our Savior through Jesus Christ our Lord, be glory, majesty, dominion, and authority, before all time and now and for ever. Amen" (Jude 24-25).

1. Jude may or may not have been one of the twelve apostles. List the "12 Apostles" below.

Matthew 10:2-4	Mark 3:16-19	Luke 6:13-16	Acts 1:13

2. To whom is the letter of Jude addressed?   Jude 1-3

3. What is Jude's purpose or reason for writing this letter?   Jude 3-4

4. Write some warnings found in the Letter of Jude.

5. What can you learn from the following verses?

Numbers 14:27-35	
1 Corinthians 10:1-5	
Hebrews 3:15-19	
Jude 5	

6. Define the term "angel." *CCC 330*

7. What is the purpose of angels? *CCC 329*

8. Who is the center of the angelic world? *CCC 331*

9. Do you have a guardian angel? Share any prayers that ask the intercession of angels?

✝

10. How could you be certain whether or not you have a guardian angel? *CCC 336*

The angels in the life of the Church

____

____

____

____

____

____

____ .   *CCC 336*

11. Jude reminds his readers of the sins of Sodom and Gomorrah. What were those sins?

Genesis 19:4-11	
Jude 7	

12. Jude 8 accuses false teachers or heretics of doing three wicked things. List them below.

13. Who contended with the devil in Jude 9?

14. Identify the angels and their roles or titles from the following passages.

Daniel 8:16	
Daniel 10:13	
Daniel 10:21	
Daniel 12:1	
Revelation 12:7	

15. Read the short book "Tobit" in your Bible and paraphrase the story.

16. Write the short wedding prayer of Tobias found in Tobit 8:5-7.

17. What are some of the duties and responsibilities of an angel? Tobit 12:11-14

Tobit 12:11-12	
Tobit 12:13	
Tobit 12:14	

✝

18. The Church celebrates the memory of three particular angels found in the Bible. Name them.

	Revelation 12:7
	Luke 1:26-31
	Tobit 12:15

19. What accusations are made in Jude 12-16?

20. Explain the exhortation given in Jude 17-19.

21. What four things should the believer do according to Jude 20-21?

22. What should the believer do for someone who doubts or wavers?   Jude 22-23

HAGGAI & ZECHARIAH 1-8
Prophets of Rebuilding

Memory Verse

"Not by might, nor by power, but by my Spirit, says the Lord of hosts."

ZECHARIAH 4:6

Very soon after his conquest of Babylon, in 538 BC, Shah Cyrus the Great of Persia issued a royal decree allowing the Jews to return to Jerusalem and rebuild their temple (Ezra 1:1-4). Other inscriptions found at different locations around the empire indicate that Cyrus was interesting in that he allowed many of the nations crushed by the Assyrians and Babylonians to restore their local temples. Cyrus did not single out the temple of Jerusalem for special favor or endowment, but created a blanket policy of restoration for those with the means to accomplish this by themselves.

Sheshbazzar led an immediate expedition to Judea to attempt rebuilding the temple but encountered too much local opposition (Ezra 4:1-5). Just as the Jews had been taken away into captivity in Babylon, other peoples had been uprooted and planted in Judea. They had adopted Jewish ways but did not belong to the blood and were not allowed to join the restored people in Judea. Eventually they formed the Samaritan nation, with their own temple on Mount Gerizim.

Meet Haggai. Before the exile, local agriculture and shepherding had formed the basis of the Judean society, despite the existence of cities. During the exile, the Jews forgot how to farm and adapted to the cosmopolitan ways of the Babylonians. When permission finally came for their return to Judea, many Jews chose to remain in the cities of the East and continued to constitute a thriving community that would contribute greatly to the development of Jewish culture, contributing among other things the famous Babylonian Talmud.

After the Babylonian exile, Jews return to Judea in four waves:

(1) Sheshbazzar in the age of Shah Cyrus the Great (after 538 BC).

(2) Zerubbabel and Jeshua lead a second wave (520 BC) during the reign of Darius I, when they successfully rebuild the temple with the encouragement of the prophets Haggai and Zechariah.

(3) Under Shah Artaxerxes I (464-423 BC), Nehemiah comes twice and succeeds in rebuilding the walls of Jerusalem.

(4) Ezra comes to codify the Mosaic law either before Nehemiah under Artaxerxes I, or after Nehemiah under Shah Artaxerxes II (404-358 BC).

When Darius I became the Shah of Shahs, supreme ruler of the Persian Empire, in the year 521 BC, conditions seemed most favorable for the rebuilding of the temple in Jerusalem. In the following year, **the prophets Haggai and Zechariah encouraged local authorities to begin work on the temple, and their prophecies are unique in having precise dates attached to them.** The Jews used the Babylonian lunar calendar, with each month having 28/29 days, but here is a rough outline of the years 520 and following to show the activity of the two prophets:

SIXTH MONTH "ELLUL" (August to September of 520 BC)
— On the first day of the new moon, Haggai's first prophecy (1:1-12)
— On the 24th day, Haggai's second prophecy (1:13-15)

SEVENTH MONTH "TISHRI" (September to October of 520 BC)
— On the 21st day, Haggai's third prophecy (2:1-9)

(Jewish New Year is now 1 Tishri in the Fall, but in Haggai's time it was in the Spring.)

EIGHTH MONTH "MARHESHVAN" (October to November of 520 BC)
— Zechariah's first prophecy (1:1-6)

NINTH MONTH "CHISLEV" (November to December of 520 BC)
— On the 24th day, Haggai's fourth and fifth prophecies (2:10-19 and 2:20-23)

ELEVENTH MONTH "SHEBAT" (January to February of 519 BC)
— On the 24th day, Zechariah's second prophecy (1:7-6:15)

TWO YEARS LATER:
NINTH MONTH "CHISLEV" (November to December of 517 BC)
— On the 4th day, Zechariah's third prophecy (7:1-7)

Temple or No Temple? The need for a temple was a debatable point within Judaism. Abraham, Isaac, Jacob, Joseph, Moses, Joshua and David had known no temple. The first temple had been a royal endowment, constructed by King Solomon and maintained by his heirs on the throne of the Southern Kingdom — but the tribes of the Northern Kingdom had not worshipped in Jerusalem. Only under one king, Solomon himself, had all Jews worshipped in one temple in Jerusalem. Therefore the Jerusalem temple could hardly be considered normative for Judaism before or during the exile.

After the exile, many Jews would have maintained that the Messiah should come first to reestablish the Kingdom of Israel, and then it would be the proper task of the Messiah himself to build the temple. If the temple is a royal institution, then it needs to have a king to establish it. Other Jews maintained that the temple should be rebuilt as soon as possible, and then the Messiah could be received there. In the meantime, while this debate went on, Jews had neither Messiah nor temple.

Into this debate come the prophets Haggai and Zechariah. Their contribution to the formation of normative Judaism is great, because of their practical advice for the community to do whatever it can under the circumstances. It is not necessary to recreate the historical circumstances of the first temple in order to build the second.

God's command to build the second temple is similar to St. Francis receiving the command to rebuild "the church." Francis thinks Christ means the church of San Damiano, but in fact Christ has in mind the whole Church. So the temple that God has in mind in Haggai's time is larger than the second temple. Later when Jesus says "Destroy this temple, and in three days I will raise it up" (John 2:19), He means not the building in Jerusalem, but the temple of His body, in which He will show His glory.

The Word of the Lord given through Haggai says: "Go up to the hills and bring wood and build the house, that I may take pleasure in it and that I may appear in my glory, says the LORD" (Haggai 1:8).

The Word of the Lord given through Zechariah says: "I have returned to Jerusalem with compassion; my house shall be built in it, says the LORD of hosts, and the measuring line shall be stretched out over Jerusalem" (Zechariah 1:16).

Meet Zechariah. The first half of the Book of Zechariah resembles the Book of Haggai in some respects. The Shah Darius appears by name again, and some of the early oracles are precisely dated. The two prophets agree on the need to rebuild the temple as a first priority.

The personalities of Zechariah and Haggai, however, are about as alike as night and day. Haggai is all business, and his prophecies contain direct and specific instructions to the Judean political leadership, in no uncertain terms. *Zechariah, on the other hand, is a dreamer and has many poetical visions.* Zechariah's first vision is dated as to month but not to day, an oversight in which Haggai would never have indulged. As the prophecies of Zechariah continue, they diverge more and more from the formula of Haggai's. From Zechariah 7:8 onwards, the prophecies are no longer dated, and from chapter nine onwards they change so drastically that many scholars consider them the work of a different prophet altogether.

It could just be, however, that Zechariah progressively throws off the prophetic forms that he received from Haggai. Zechariah may have been a disciple of Haggai, but in the course of time, he becomes more like the prophets of old rather than like his own master. We already know that Haggai's prophecies all took place within a single year, while Zechariah's dated prophecies spanned several years. Zechariah may have continued prophesying to span the gap until the arrival of Nehemiah under the reign of Artaxerxes I (464-423 BC).

Zechariah and the Horses ~ The great empires of high antiquity based their power largely upon their cavalries. From the Mongolian desert, where the horse was probably first domesticated during the second millennium BC, came wave after wave of barbarian invaders, of different races and cultures. The Hurrians brought horsepower into the Middle East, and by the time of Moses the cavalry was the backbone of Egyptian military power. The Arabs bred horses whose swiftness could carry them across the harsh conditions of the deep desert, while other breeds could work the fields or be hitched to surreys. The biblical image of the horse, however, is principally related to the arts of war and not the arts of peace.

Zechariah's second oracle contains four horses, two colored red, one sorrel and one white, which God has sent to patrol the earth. The oracle only mentions a horseman on one of the red horses, but clearly the other three have riders also (Zechariah 1:8-11). Later in the same book, Zechariah describes four chariots with horses that are red, black, white and dappled gray (Zechariah 6:2-3). Both the four horsemen and the four charioteers are only observers; they are like symbols of the omniscience of God and do not have the active role in the end times that the Four Horsemen of the Apocalypse have:

> **I saw, and behold, a white horse, and its rider had a bow; and a crown was given to him, and he went out conquering and to conquer (Revelation 6:2).**
>
> **[O]ut came another horse, bright red; its rider was permitted to take peace from the earth, so that men should slay one another; and he was given a great sword (Revelation 6:4).**
>
> **I saw, and behold, a black horse, and its rider had a balance in his hand; and I heard what seemed to be a voice in the midst of the four living creatures saying, "A quart of wheat for a denarius, and three quarts of barley for a denarius; but do not harm oil and wine!" (Revelation 6:5-6).**
>
> **I saw, and behold, a pale horse, and its rider's name was Death, and Hades followed him; and they were given power over a fourth of the earth, to kill with sword and with famine and with pestilence and by wild beasts of the earth (Revelation 6:8).**

Zechariah's two sets of four horses do not have the same coloration as the four horses of Revelation either, but the notion of four colored horses clearly constitutes part of the language of apocalyptic writing, through the five hundred year period separating these two biblical authors.

Other apocalyptic images appear for the first time in the Book of Zechariah but continue to be developed in later authors. Zechariah presents an image of four horns (Zechariah 1:18), and Daniel includes an image of ten horns (Daniel 7:19-21). Zechariah introduces the image of a measuring line (Zechariah 2:1), which is also found in the Books of Ezekiel (40:3-4) and Revelation (21:15-17). Zechariah sees a seven-branched candlestick (Zechariah 4:2) and the Book of Revelation introduces us to the seven churches, which are spread out on the geography of the Aegean Basin like a menorah (Revelation 1-2).

Both Haggai and Zechariah urged the building of the second temple, and contributed to Judaism's understanding of the temple as an institution. Zechariah did even more; he invented the basic language of Jewish apocalyptic symbolism, which would give great service in subsequent composition of the Bible.

1. Compare the following verses. Who suggests what?

2 Samuel 7:1-2	
Haggai 1:3-4	

2. What can be learned from the following passages?

Deuteronomy 28:38-45	
Micah 6:15	
Haggai 1:5-6	

3. Who destroyed the temple in Jerusalem?   2 Kings 25:8-17

4. Compare the following passages.

Genesis 27:28	
Amos 4:6-9	
Haggai 1:7-11	

5. How did the people respond to the words spoken through Haggai?   Haggai 1:12, 14

6. Write the Word of the Lord in the following verses.

Haggai 1:13	
Haggai 2:4	
Matthew 28:20	

7. What was the relationship between behavior and quality of life described in Haggai 1:5-11?

8. What is promised in Haggai 2:1-9?

9. Explain the problem in Haggai 2:10-14.

10. Compare the following verses.

Exodus 15:1	
Haggai 2:22	
Zechariah 14:13-15	
Luke 1:52	

11. Compare the following verses.

Song of Songs 8:6	
Sirach 49:11	
Isaiah 44:1-5	
Haggai 2:23	

12. What does the Lord ask in the following passages?

Isaiah 55:6-9	
Hosea 14:1-7	
Amos 5:4-7	
Zechariah 1:2-6	

13. Compare the images in the following verses.

Ezekiel 40:3-4	
Zechariah 2:1	
Revelation 21:15-17	

14. Is the measuring line in Zechariah meant for devastation or reconstruction?

15. Compare the following verses.

Psalm 29:2	
Psalm 96:2	
Psalm 113:1-2	
Zechariah 2:13-17	

16. What do you know about the name of the Lord? *CCC 2143*

CCC 2143

17. Describe the drama in Zechariah 3:1-10 in your own words.

18. Identify the major characters in Zechariah 4 and their dialogue.

19. Compare the following verses.

Zechariah 4:1-2	
Revelation 1:12	
Zechariah 4:3, 11-12	
Revelation 11:4	

20. Describe two visions in chapter 5. Find one word from Zechariah 5:8 to explain these.

21. Compare the following two visions.

Zechariah 6:1-8	*Revelation 6:2-8*

22. What does the Lord command in Zechariah 6:12-15?

23. What does the Lord desire from the people in Zechariah 7:9-10? How do they respond?
Verses 11-12

24. Compare the following verses.

Nahum 1:2	
Zechariah 8:2	
Isaiah 2:2	
Zechariah 8:3	
Isaiah 11:11	
Jeremiah 30:18	
Zechariah 8:7-8	

25. What does the Lord command in Zechariah 8:16-17?

26. What does the Lord foretell for the future? Zechariah 8:20-23?

ZECHARIAH 7-14
Your King Comes

Memory Verse

**"And I will pour out on the house of David and the inhabitants of Jerusalem
a spirit of compassion and supplication,
so that, when they look on him whom they have pierced,
they shall mourn for him, as one mourns for an only child,
and weep bitterly over him, as one weeps over a first-born."**

ZECHARIAH 12:10

The Book of Zechariah contributed greatly to the expectation of the coming of a Messiah. Three New Testament authors—Paul, Matthew and John—incorporate direct quotations from the second half of this book, which they use to identify Jesus as the anointed King whom this prophet foresaw.

The Essence of Prophetic Morality ~ Several prophetic and apostolic authors attempt to summarize the essence of biblical moral teaching, as in the famous passage: "[W]hat does the Lord require of you but to do justice, and to love kindness, and to walk humbly with your God?" (Micah 6:8). In the seventh and eighth chapters of his book, Zechariah passes on to us a couple of similarly eloquent passages:

Render true judgments, show kindness and mercy each to his brother, do not oppress the widow, the fatherless, the sojourner, or the poor; and let none of you devise evil against his brother in your heart.
                    (Zechariah 7:9-10)
	These are the things that you shall do: Speak the truth to one another, render in your gates judgments that are true and make for peace, do not devise evil in your hearts against one another, and love no false oath.
	                    (Zechariah 8:16-17

These passages go beyond the minimum observation of the Mosaic commandment, "You shall not bear false witness against your neighbor" (Exodus 20:16, and Deuteronomy 6:20). That commandment is phrased negatively, and forbids us to commit the sin of perjury to the harm of another person. Zechariah's version is phrased positively, and requires us to step forward and tell the truth if it can be of help to our neighbor. To withhold the truth can be just as bad as proferring a lie. That is why one swears in the court of law to tell "the truth, the whole truth and nothing but the truth." A half truth can be one full lie.

St. Paul studied these beautiful passages and inserts a quotation from one of them into his treatment of the nature of the Church in the Letter to the Ephesians: "Therefore, putting away falsehood, let everyone speak the truth with his neighbor, for we are members of one another" (Ephesians 4:25). The unity of the body requires that all of the members act in coordination with one another. The hand cannot withhold information from the heart, and vice versa. Within the Mystical Body of Christ, likewise, the truth must be told. Those preaching must speak fearlessly, those exchanging vows must do so without reservation, and those confessing their sins must withhold no serious matter. The instinct to project a false image to the world around us must be set aside. Zechariah and Paul are of one accord on this subject—the good of society and the good of the Church require heroic honesty on the part of individual members. Anything less would be an injustice.

In our time, honesty sometimes becomes an excuse for rudeness. We do not have to wound one another's feelings in the process of telling the truth. Zechariah puts it so beautifully: "Render in your gates judgments that are true and make for peace, do not devise evil in your hearts against one another." If words do not make for peace, are they really true? If words express evil in the heart, is this what we really mean by honesty?

The Humble Coming of a King ~ At the beginning of chapter 9, Zechariah's oracles' take on a poetic form. Until now they have been prosaic, but now they appear in typical Hebrew doublets. Verse 9 illustrates the parallelism:
> "Rejoice greatly, O daughter of Zion!
> Shout aloud, O daughter of Jerusalem!" (Zechariah 9:9a).

See how the word "daughter" repeats in each sentence. "Zion" is a synonym for "Jerusalem." "Rejoice greatly" and "shout aloud" are roughly equivalent. This kind of doubling composition is one of the key distinguishing characteristics of Hebrew poetry. That same verse continues in the same doubling way, and presents one of the most important prophecies of the Messiah:
> "Lo, your king comes to you;
> triumphant and victorious is he,
> humble and riding on an ass,
> on a colt the foal of an ass" (Zechariah 9:9a).

This verse looks clear enough, but apparently there was quite a bit of discussion among ancient Jews about how many donkeys appear in this verse. Is there one donkey, mentioned twice, or are there two distinct donkeys. Hebrew verse lays itself open for this kind of problem with its doubling style. Sometimes there really were two different things, but sometimes just one thing said twice.

The Evangelist John seems to think there is just one donkey, because in his account of Palm Sunday he writes: "So they took branches of palm trees and went out to meet him, crying, 'Hosanna! Blessed is he who comes in the name of the Lord, even the King of Israel!' And Jesus found a young ass and sat upon it; as it is written, 'Fear not, daughter of Zion; behold, your King is coming, sitting on an ass's colt!'" (John 12:13-14).

The Evangelist Matthew, in his parallel account, remembers a second donkey: "Jesus sent two disciples, saying to them, 'Go into the village opposite you, and immediately you will find an ass tied, and a colt with her; untie them and bring them to me. If anyone says anything to you, you shall say, "'The Lord has need of them," and he will send them immediately.' This took place to fulfil what was spoken by the prophet saying, 'Tell the daughter of Zion, Behold, your King is coming to you, humble, and mounted on an ass, and on a colt, the foal of an ass.' The disciples went and did as Jesus had directed them; they brought the ass and the colt, and put their garments on them, and He sat thereon" (Matthew 21:1-7).

Now clearly Jesus can only sit on one animal at a time, and the colt is only there for window dressing. Nonetheless, Jesus wishes to give a clear signal that His entrance into Jerusalem is the fulfillment of Zechariah's prophecy, so for the benefit of the literally minded He orders a second donkey as part of the Palm Sunday procession.

Donkeys have practically disappeared from use in first-world countries, but remain important elsewhere. Montana rancher John Steffen worked with donkeys in Australia and believes the phrase "on an ass, on a colt the foal of an ass" suggests purity of bloodline. Donkeys can mate with horses, but the resulting offspring is a barren mule. On Palm Sunday, the tethered foal proved that the she-donkey upon which Jesus rode was purebred, to satisfy the requirements of prophecy.

It is not difficult harmonizing the two accounts. The existence of a second historical donkey on Palm Sunday is not a burning questions, but what is of interest is the relative importance that the Evangelists give it. Matthew seems to feel that the second donkey was important, while John doesn't. Maybe they were thinking of their readers, and Matthew's Jewish audience was accustomed to reading the prophets quite literally.

Clearly both Matthew and John, the two evangelists who were eye-witnesses, understand the events of the first Holy Week as fulfillment of the messianic prophecies of Zechariah. We would be wrong to think that only many decades later, as they sat down to write their Gospels, the two of them wanted to forge some prophetic link. Rather, as they stood before Jesus on the original Palm Sunday, from their own study, they saw Jesus as the fulfillment of prophecy. The message of Zechariah was ingrained in the hearts and minds of those who yearned for the coming of the Messiah. That was why Jesus wanted them to get two donkeys—so that it would be absolutely clear to the most literally minded among them that He Himself is the Messiah, the Christ.

Negative Prototype: The Worthless Shepherd ~ In chapter 11, Zechariah pretends to be a worthless shepherd who does not care about the sheep. He enacts a prophetic drama, in which he abandons and betrays a flock of sheep. He goes on to take his wage, thirty pieces of silver, and he casts it into the treasury of the temple as a donation. Why thirty pieces of silver? Because according to the Mosaic law, this is the redemptory price of a slave: "If the ox gores a slave, male or female, the owner shall give to their master thirty shekels of silver, and the ox shall be stoned" (Exodus 21:32).

The buying and selling of human beings is something intrinsically abhorrent to us, but the sad fact is that through most of human history people have been willing to buy other people. Now some slaves are more valuable to their owners than others; some can do more work or have special skills that would allow their price to be higher in the slave market. In the ancient slave trade, there was haggling between buyer and seller over each slave that was up for sale. The Mosaic law acknowledges that if a slave is accidentally killed by an ox, the slave owner will want to claim as high a value as the market could bear, while the ox-driver would want to pay as low a value. The law proposes a standard formula in order to keep peace between

the owner of the slave and the owner of the ox. Intrinsically, each person's life is of equally inestimable value, but the Mosaic law settles upon thirty silver shekels (plus the value of the slaughtered ox) as the practical value of a dead slave.

Matthew draws elements from the prophecies of Jeremiah and of Zechariah in describing the fate of Judas Iscariot, who betrayed the Good Shepherd and allowed Him to be destroyed:
"And they paid him thirty pieces of silver" (Matthew 26:15).
"And throwing down the pieces of silver in the temple, he departed" (Matthew 27:9).

To the original readers of Matthew's Gospel, the words of Zechariah would have echoed in the association with Judas: "What is to die, let it die; what is to be destroyed, let it be destroyed" (Zechariah 11:9). Judas let Jesus die and took his own life as well. By contrast, Jesus says, "The thief comes only to steal and kill and destroy; I came that they may have life and have it abundantly" (John 10:10). Zechariah allows himself to act the part of a negative prototype, foreshadowing Judas. Jesus takes the part of the positive archetype, that of the Good Shepherd.

Positive Prototype: The Stricken Shepherd ~ Zechariah belongs to the same school of thought as Isaiah, who taught the doctrine of the Suffering Servant. They foretold that the coming Messiah would have to suffer in order to usher in the Kingdom of God. The necessity of Christ's Passion is a clear prophetic message.

So Zechariah records this message: "Awake, O sword, against my shepherd, against the man who stands next to me, says the Lord of hosts. Strike the shepherd, that the sheep may be scattered" (Zechariah 13:7). On Holy Thursday night, within hearing of the Evangelist Matthew on the Mount of Olives, Jesus connects this verse with Himself: "Jesus said to them, 'You will all fall away from me this night; for it is written, "'I will strike the shepherd, and the sheep of the flock will be scattered'"'" (Matthew 26:31).

Likewise Zechariah writes, "I will pour out on the house of David and the inhabitants of Jerusalem a spirit of compassion and supplication, so that, when they look on him whom they have pierced, they shall mourn for him, as one mourns for an only child, and weep bitterly over him, as one weeps over a first born" (Zechariah 12:10). This prophecy is fulfilled first when Mary wept over the broken body of her Son—but she was not guilty of having pierced Him. John, on the other hand, who was there supporting Mary on that occasion, looked upon the broken body of the one who had died for his, John's, own salvation, for the forgiveness of John's own sins. Later, in his own Gospel, John cites Zechariah's verse to explain what he himself saw, alone of all twelve apostles: "[A]nother scripture says, They shall look on him whom they have pierced" (John 19:34, 37).

One good Catholic woman, after seeing the movie *The Passion of the Christ*, said she wondered how much of Christ's suffering had been made necessary because of her sins. The truth is that Christ values each of us so much that He would have been willing to offer all of that suffering for just one of us. Saint Thomas Aquinas believed that there was so much intrinsic value in the Blood of Christ that one drop would have been enough to save the world, and all the rest was merely a gracious display of divine generosity.

Mary and John mourned for the Messiah as His body was being taken down from the Cross. Though our faults made it necessary, we mourn long afterwards. Zechariah mourned in advance.

1. How were the people confronted in Zechariah 7:1-7?

2. What does the Lord prefer to fasting?   Zechariah 7:8-10

3. How did the people respond to the Word of the Lord?   Zechariah 7:11-14

4. Describe in your own words, the Word of the Lord in Zechariah 8:1-15.

5. What should you do according to Zechariah 8:16-17?

6. Explain some of the disasters that will befall Israel's enemies? Zechariah 9:1-8

7. Compare the following verses.

Zechariah 9:9	
Matthew 21:5	
John 12:14-15	

8. How will Jerusalem welcome her Messiah? *CCC 559*

9. What will happen to Israel according to Zechariah 9:11-17?

10. What can you learn from comparing the following verses?

Zechariah 10:1-2	
Zechariah 14:17	
Joel 2:18-27	
Amos 4:7-8	

11. To what do the following passages point?

Isaiah 43:1-7, 14-21	
Jeremiah 23:3	
Hosea 11:11	
Zechariah 10:8-12	

12. Compare the shepherds in the following verses.

Zechariah 11:7-14	
John 10:1, 8-13	

13. To what does the oracle in Zechariah 12:1-9 point?

14. To whom do the following verses point?

Isaiah 52:12-53:12	
Zechariah 12:10-14	
Matthew 23:37	
John 19:34-37	
Revelation 1:7	

15. How is the human heart converted? *CCC 1432*

____

____

____

____

____

____

____

____. *CCC 1432*

16. What is the appropriate response of the human person to God? *CCC 2561*

17. Compare these verses.

Psalm 46:4	
Zechariah 13:1	
Revelation 22:1-2	

18. Compare Zechariah 13:7 with Matthew 26:31 and Mark 14:27.

19. What activity is foretold in Zechariah chapter 14?

20. What hope can you derive from Zechariah 14:9?

1 PETER
First Papal Encyclical

Memory Verse

**"All flesh is like grass and all its glory like the flower of grass.
The grass withers, and the flower falls,
but the word of the Lord abides forever."**

1 PETER 1:24-25

Saint Peter, primary among the apostles and our first pope writes the first papal encyclical to encourage the early Church. Peter recalls the Passion of Jesus Christ, by which He suffered and died to atone for the sins of the world. He encourages Christians to suffer as well, in hope and joy, anticipating an ultimate reward in heaven. Baptism, which saves the soul of the repentant sinner, constitutes both a gift and a call. The suffering of Christ gives meaning to human suffering and guides the moral conduct of Christians, who desire to imitate Christ in being servants of all.

Meet Peter. Simon Peter, son of Jonah, was a fisherman on the Sea of Galilee. Originally from Bethsaida, Peter lived in Capernaum. We know that Peter was married at one time, because Jesus healed his mother-in-law (Matthew 8:14-15). While Jesus walked on the shore, he saw Peter and Andrew fishing on the lake of Genessaret and He said to them, "Follow me, and I will make you fishers of men" (Matthew 4:19). Immediately, they left their nets to follow Jesus, providing a perfect example for believers of all time.

"Peter, an apostle of Jesus Christ" is a phrase which reveals the author's humility but also teaches something about the papacy. Peter was head of the apostles, but also one of their number. In the same way, popes are "primus inter pares," first among equals. The Second Vatican Council taught the collegiality of all bishops together, including the pope. The pope is the head of the universal Church, but he must first be the Bishop of Rome. Jesus called Peter an apostle first and then named him the rock. Only an apostle could be Peter, and only a bishop can be pope.

Peter enjoys preeminence among the twelve apostles, even during the lifetime of Jesus. Jesus reveals His power to Peter in a way that Peter can clearly understand with the miraculous catch of fish. Peter may not have known a lot about some things, but he knew a great deal about fishing. When he saw the huge catch, after toiling unsuccessfully all night, Peter recognized that he was in the presence of the Divine. Simon Peter demonstrated a perfect response to the God-Man, Jesus Christ. He fell at Jesus' knees, saying, "Depart from me, for I am a sinful man, O Lord" (Luke 5:8).

Silvanus helped compose this letter with its excellent Greek, of which Peter was not a native speaker. At letter's end, Peter names among his companions another excellent scribe, "my son Mark," who will later become famous as one of the four evangelists. Scholars believe Mark's Gospel is a record of Peter's own preaching. Peter contributes to the biblical conversation about faith and works: "As the outcome of your faith you obtain the salvation of your souls" (1 Peter 1:9). Although Peter and Paul did not always see eye-to-eye, Peter here

seems to agree with Paul. If faith is the first step of our journey and salvation the last one, there still may be many necessary steps between.

Peter writes to "the exiles in the Dispersion," people of Jewish origin who had converted to the love of Jesus. Since their youth, his readers had studied the prophets, who worked not for themselves but for those who would follow. Peter quotes Isaiah, who illustrated universal mortality by means of the flowers of the field, but then declared the Word of the Lord immune from death. We only exist in the first place because God says so, and we shall exist forever by that same power.

"You are the Christ, the Son of the living God" (Matthew 16:15). Following Peter's exquisite profession of faith, Jesus gives him a nickname. In the Bible, a new name connotes a commission from God. Abram becomes Abraham. Jacob becomes Israel. Jesus calls Peter "Kepha," an Aramaic word meaning "rock," translated "Petros" in Greek. Since Peter (or Cephas) can also be translated "stone," observe Peter developing the imagery of the spiritual rock in chapter 2.

The **"Four Marks of the True Church"** evolve from Peter's speech about living stones:
One ~ Unity builds the stones together into an edifice of spirit.
Holy ~ Holiness develops because the unity brings sanctification, as a "holy dwelling."
Catholic ~ Catholicity allows the many to retain their individuality while being built into something bigger than themselves. The Church has room for everyone of every nation and race.
Apostolic ~ The apostles are the foundation of this structure, and Peter, the rock himself is speaking in this passage to invite all later generations to share in the apostolic tradition.

Jesus builds His Church on Peter, the rock and promises that the powers of death will not prevail against it. The Old Testament prophet Isaiah promised, "I will place on his shoulder the key of the house of David; he shall open, and none shall shut; and he shall shut, and none shall open" (Isaiah 22:23). Jesus offers the New Testament fulfillment of this prophecy when He says, "I will give you the keys of the kingdom of heaven, and whatever you bind on earth shall be bound in heaven, and whatever you loose on earth shall be loosed in heaven" (Matthew 16:19).

In Christian art and sculpture, a figure with keys in his hands depicts Peter, the keeper of the keys. Before St. Peter's Basilica in Rome, enormous statues of Peter and Paul stand on either side of the entrance, and St. Peter is the one holding the keys. Inside St. Peter's, after passing Michelangelo's Pieta and the Adoration Chapel, there is a bronze sculpture of a seated St. Peter, from an unknown 4th century Syrian sculptor. Pilgrims kiss or touch the feet of this statue, and in doing so have worn St. Peter's foot to a smooth surface. The sacristy of St. Peter's rises above the Scavi, housing the bones of Peter. Tradition tells us that Peter was martyred by crucifixion between 64-67 AD. Protesting that he was unworthy to die as Jesus did, Peter asked to be crucified upside down.

The Petrine authority through two millennia has clarified issues of doctrine when heresies and errors arose. Catholics find comfort in Jesus' words in Matthew 16:18-19 when seeking the Church of Christ and alleviation from the guilt of their sins. The penitent, confessing his sins to God through the priest in confession rejoices in hearing the words of absolution and recalls the words of Jesus assuring him that his sins, which have been loosed on earth, are also loosed in heaven. When there are questions of faith and morals, if you don't know what to do or whom to believe, look to Peter, and his successor, the pope.

Despite Peter's three-fold denial of our Lord, which Jesus foretold, Peter repented and never lost his place of preeminence. After the Resurrection, an angel tells the women at the tomb to tell Peter that Jesus is going to Galilee and will meet them there (Mark 16:7). Following Peter's three betrayals of Jesus, Our Lord asks him three times if he loves Him and commissions Peter three times to feed His sheep. Jesus also prepared Peter for the martyrdom by which he would glorify God.

Following Jesus' Ascension into heaven, the Holy Spirit empowers Peter to fulfill the role for which he was called. Peter prompts the apostles to find a replacement for Judas, and Peter speaks boldly at Pentecost, "Repent and be baptized, every one of you, in the name of Jesus Christ for the forgiveness of your sins" (Acts 2:38). Peter's preaching brought three thousand believers to the Church in one day! Despite his faults, recorded in the Bible, Peter remains the keeper of the keys. In the debate over the circumcision of Gentile Christians, it is Peter who settles the dispute at the Council in Jerusalem (Acts 15:7-11). Peter has spoken! And later he pens this beautiful letter.

The First Letter of Peter focuses on suffering. Twelve times the verb "suffer" is used and another four times the noun "suffering" appears in 1 Peter. Of all the references to suffering in the New Testament, more than one fourth of them come from this letter. The Catholic concept of redemptive suffering emerges in this letter. Catholic school children have been taught to "offer it up" when encountering trials or difficulties. Adults with serious health problems, marital or financial difficulties are encouraged to "rejoice in so far as you share Christ's suffering" (1 Peter 4:13). While trials and sufferings come to all men, they can be met with denial and anger or with quiet resignation and peace. Those sufferings joined with the sufferings of Christ can accomplish some ultimate good.

The Passion of our Lord Jesus Christ and the power of His Resurrection from the dead bring the believer in touch with God's great mercy. St. Peter repeats again and again the importance of the suffering of Jesus for the sins of the world (1 Peter 1:11, 2:21, 2:23, 3:18, 4:1, 5:1). Peter reminds Christians that they were "ransomed . . . with the precious blood of Christ, like that of a lamb without blemish or spot" (1 Peter 1:18-19). In the Hebrew Scriptures, the concept of sacrifice requires the blood of a perfect, unblemished Passover Lamb (Exodus 12:5-13).

"The blood of Christ, while it reveals the grandeur of the Father's love, shows how precious man is in God's eyes and how priceless the value of his life. The Apostle Peter reminds us of this: "You know that you were ransomed from the futile ways inherited from your fathers, not with perishable things such as silver or gold, but with the precious blood of Christ, like that of a lamb without blemish or spot" (1 Peter 1:18-19). Precisely by contemplating the precious blood of Christ, the sign of His self-giving love (cf. John 13:1), the believer learns to recognize and appreciate the almost divine dignity of every human being and can exclaim with ever renewed and grateful wonder: "How precious must man be in the eyes of the Creator, if he 'gained so great a Redeemer' (Exsultet of the Easter Vigil), and if God 'gave His only Son' in order that man 'should not perish but have eternal life!' " (John 3:16).

Furthermore, Christ's blood reveals to man that his greatness, and therefore his vocation, consists in the sincere gift of self ... Whoever in the Sacrament of the Eucharist drinks this blood and abides in Jesus (cf. John 6:56) is drawn into the dynamism of His love and gift of life, in order to bring to its fullness the original vocation to love which belongs to everyone."

Pope John Paul II, *Evangelium Vitae,* (March 25, 1999), no. 25.3-4.

Beautiful lyric verses from 1 Peter 2:9-10 show the fulfillment of four Old Testament concepts. A chosen race (Isaiah 43:20-21) and royal priesthood (Exodus 19:6) show the Christians as divinely elected to worship and serve God. God desires a "holy nation" and "God's own people" (Malachi 3:17) who come out of the darkness of sin and separation into the wonderful light of His mercy and steadfast love. St. Peter offers baptism to reconcile the sinner to God and reminds the believer that he has "been born anew through the living and abiding word of God" (1 Peter 1:23).

Christians, strangers and sojourners in this world, must wage war against the passions of the flesh. Peter encourages husbands and wives to live peaceably and win souls by their reverent behavior. Wives should develop "the hidden person of the heart with the imperishable jewel of a gentle and quiet spirit, which in God's sight is very precious" (1 Peter 3:4). Marital harmony provides a witness of God's love to unbelievers and increases the possibility of God hearing prayers.

Christian conduct involves striving for unity of spirit, being humble, tenderhearted and loving one another. Peter admonishes the believers, "Do not return evil for evil" (1 Peter 3:9). "Above all hold unfailing your love for one another, since love covers a multitude of sins" (1 Peter 4:8). Peter knew Jesus and saw His steadfast love poured out in service to others. Jesus washed Peter's feet and commanded "love one another; even as I have loved you, that you also love one another. By this all men will know that you are my disciples, if you love one another" (John 13:34-35).

Peter's job is to make disciples of all nations and to build up Christ's Church. The early Christian community was known by its love and service toward one another, the poor and the downtrodden. The task of the Christian is to become holy and be holy in all conduct (1 Peter 1:15).

> But because He Himself said, 'Be holy, as I too am holy' (1 Peter 1:16; Leviticus 20:7), we ask and seek that very thing, so that we who have been made holy in Baptism may persevere in what we have begun to be. For this we do daily pray. We have a daily need of being made holy, so that we who sin daily may be cleansed again of our sins by continual sanctification … we pray that this sanctification may abide in us.
> St. Cyprian of Carthage (+258 AD), *Treatise on the Lord's Prayer*, 12.

Peter cautions his "beloved" flock not to be surprised at the fiery ordeal that comes, as though something strange were happening. "But rejoice in so far as you may share Christ's sufferings, that you may also rejoice and be glad when his glory is revealed" (1 Peter 4:12). Since the Master suffered, the disciples must expect to suffer also. The believer who joins his suffering to that of Christ will receive grace to bear it and ultimately experience peace and joy!

Practical advice involves humbling yourself that God may exalt you, casting your anxieties on Him, and doing spiritual warfare. Resist evil. St. Peter retells the Passion of Jesus Christ in which the Innocent One suffered for the guilty. He offers testimony to the grace of God that allows believers to live a new life of hope and joy. Peter presents a defense for the hope that he has experienced, since the Lord Jesus Christ had transformed a humble fisherman into the "Rock of the Church," and the "Keeper of the Keys."

1. Read the First Letter of Peter and write your favorite verse below.

2. What can you learn about Peter from the following? *CCC 552*

Simon Peter holds the ____

____

____

____

____

____

____

____

____

____

____

____. *CCC 552*

3. What does the "power of the keys" designate? *CCC 553*

4. What has Jesus given?   1 Peter 1:3-5

5. Explain the Paschal mystery. 1 Peter 1:3, *CCC 654*

6. "Faith tested by fire" (1 Peter 1:7) refers to what reality? *CCC 1031*

7. Who foretold "the grace to be yours?" 1 Peter 1:10-12

8. Compare the following verses.

Leviticus 11:44-45
1 Peter 1:15-16

9. How is one born anew? What lasts forever? 1 Peter 1:23-25

10. What enables the Word of God to produce its life-giving effect? 1 Peter 3:21, *CCC 1228*

11. Compare the following verses.

Psalm 118:22	
Isaiah 28:16	
Matthew 21:42	
1 Peter 2:4-6	

12. Where should one see the participation of "a chosen race, a royal priesthood?"
1 Peter 2:9 ***CCC 1141***

13. List some obligations of Christians from the following passages.

1 Peter 2:12	
1 Peter 2:17	
1 Peter 3:1	
1 Peter 3:7	
1 Peter 3:8-9	
1 Peter 3:15	
1 Peter 4:8-9	
1 Peter 5:5-6	
1 Peter 5:8-9	

14. Explain the difficult concept presented in 1 Peter 3:19. *CCC 632*

15. How could you apply 1 Peter 3:15 to your personal life?

16. How can you make sense out of suffering?

1 Peter 4:1-2	
1 Peter 4:12-13	

17. What does Peter advise in the following passages?

1 Peter 2:11	
1 Peter 5:8-9	

18. Is the devil (Satan) real? *CCC 2851,   CCC 2852*

19. Describe the battle that you are in.   1 Peter 5:8,   *CCC 409*

20. How can you achieve victory in the battle with evil?   1 Peter 5:9, *CCC 2849*

Monthly Social Activity

This month your small group will meet for coffee, tea, or a simple breakfast or lunch in someone's home.

Pray for this social event and for the host or hostess. Try if at all possible to attend. Offer hospitality for one of the socials to be held at your home.

The first apostles were evangelists, sharing the Good News.

Now reflect on your own personal life.

~ What are some ways you can share your faith with others?

~ Have you ever had a positive experience in sharing your faith?

~ Could your small group consider ways of reaching out to others?

~ List some people you could pray for and invite to the Bible study.

2 PETER
Christ Will Come Again

Memory Verse

**"But do not ignore this one fact, beloved,
that with the Lord one day is as a thousand years,
and a thousand years as one day.
The Lord is not slow about his promise as some count slowness,
but is forbearing toward you,
not wishing that any should perish, but that all should reach repentance."**

2 PETER 3:8-9

The Second Letter of Peter warns Christians to avoid false teachers and their heresies and reaffirms our faith and hope in the truth of the Second Coming of Jesus Christ in glory (the parousia). On all Sundays and solemnities, Catholics proclaim this truth in the Profession of Faith at Mass:

"We believe in one Lord, Jesus Christ . . .
For us men and for our salvation He came down from heaven:
By the power of the Holy Spirit He was born of the Virgin Mary, and became man.
For our sake He was crucified under Pontius Pilate:
He suffered, died, and was buried.
On the third day He rose again in fulfillment of the Scriptures;
He ascended into heaven and is seated at the right hand of the Father.
*He will come again in glory to judge the living and the dead,
and His kingdom will have no end."*

Peter, the servant and apostle of our Lord Jesus Christ, wants to remind the Church about the importance of this truth of the faith at the twilight of his life. Jesus has advised Peter that his days on this earth are drawing to a close, and he desires to strengthen the body in the truth before he departs. "I think it right, as long as I am in this body, to arouse you by way of reminder, since I know that the putting off of my body will be soon, as our Lord Jesus Christ showed me" (2 Peter 1:13-14). This apostle wants to make sure that the believers are secure in the fullness of truth and can rely on a written record after his death.

The Transfiguration points to Jesus' future coming in glory. False teachers develop cleverly concocted myths in every time and generation. "I'm OK, you're OK." "A loving God would never send anyone to hell." "My God doesn't really care what you do as long as you're sincere." "That was the Old Testament God. Mine is the New." Guess what! There is only one true God. The God of the Old Testament is the God of the New Testament. God is omnipotent, omniscience, all-loving, all-just, eternal, unchanging. While God may reveal more of Himself or different aspects of His divine nature to people at different times, He doesn't change! The apostles were eyewitnesses of the majesty of God. Peter, James and John were honored by Jesus in being invited up the mountain for the Transfiguration (Matthew 17:1-8, Mark 9:2-8, Luke 9:28-36). They heard the voice of God the Father from heaven, and they beheld the glory of the Son of God!

The apostle asserts that "His divine power has granted to us all things that pertain to life and godliness, through the knowledge of him who called us to his own glory and excellence, by which he has granted to us his precious and very great promises, that through these you may escape from the corruption that is in the world because of passion, and become partakers of the divine nature" (2 Peter 1:3-4). Perhaps the early Christians grew weary waiting for the return of the Lord. Perhaps some became vulnerable to the contemporary slogans and slick gimmicks of the false teachers of their day. How do you obtain His divine power and partake of more of the divine nature?

With full confidence, partake of the Body and Blood of Christ . . . So that by partaking of the Body and Blood of Christ, you might become united in body and blood with Him. For thus do we become Christ-bearers, His Body and Blood being distributed through our members. And thus it is that we become, according to the blessed Peter, sharers of the divine nature.

St. Cyril of Jerusalem (315-386 AD), *Mystagogic*, 4.3.

Flight from the world *(Fuga Mundi)* inspired many Christians to embark upon monastic life, removed from the passions and temptations of the world. "The world" here represents that corrupt sphere under the temporary domain of the evil one. God created the world and all its beauty and goodness. However, the world, the flesh and the devil seek to lure the child of God away from the fullness of joy devised by God according to His purposes. God sent Jesus to save mankind from sin and offer eternal life. Grace is poured out to animate knowledge and faith in God into moral virtues and a growth in holiness. The goal of every Christian is to become a saint!

In the language of the Bible 'grace' means a special gift, which according to the New Testament has its source precisely in the Trinitarian life of God Himself, God who is love (John 4:8). The fruit of this love is "the election" of which the Letter to the Ephesians speaks. On the part of God, this election is the eternal desire to save man through a sharing in His own life (2 Peter 1:4) in Christ: it is salvation through a sharing in supernatural life. The effect of this eternal gift, of this grace of man's election by God, is like a seed of holiness, or a spring which rises in the soul as a gift from God Himself, who through grace gives life and holiness to those who are chosen.

Pope John Paul II, *Redemptoris Mater* (March 25, 1987), no. 8.4.

The Christian places total faith and trust in the Lord Jesus Christ and receives grace from God to grow in holiness. Peter admonishes the believer to "make every effort" to supplement your faith with virtue and knowledge. Free will, the gift of God, presupposes that conscious choice and effort must be exerted to grow in virtue and holiness. Self-control, steadfastness, controlling passions and desires, godliness and brotherly love are required to be fruitful for the Lord Jesus Christ. The Christian who strives to control unruly passions and grow in virtue and holiness can become a fruitful witness for the Lord. How to achieve this? "[B]e the more zealous to confirm your call and election, for if you do this you will never fall" (2 Peter 1:10).

"[N]o prophecy of scripture is a matter of one's own interpretation because no prophecy ever came by the impulse of man, but men moved by the Holy Spirit spoke from God" (2 Peter 1:20). Many believe that the Bible is the inspired Word of God. However, many also interpret Bible passages to mean vastly different things. The understanding of biblical inspiration and hermeneutics practiced by the early Church and continuing through the centuries contains three major principles:

1) All Scripture is prophetic because it is truth revealed by God.

2) The inspired words of the Old Testament prophets, "scripture," and the inspired words of the New Testament apostles, "the prophetic word," illustrated here in the Transfiguration compared with the Second Coming, can only be interpreted under the guidance of the Holy Spirit (2 Peter 1:19).

3) Correct interpretation provided by the Holy Spirit requires the authoritative discernment of the apostolic church—Peter and his successors writing in Peter's name (Petrine authority).

False prophets and false teachers can be clearly identified in a number of ways. Bold and arrogant, they draw attention to themselves, rather than pointing to Jesus. They glorify themselves rather than giving glory to God. Greed manifests itself in the life of the heretic. The love of money and desire for power or fame raises a red flag. Finally, revelry, adultery and carousing provide an ungodly witness. The true prophet, on the contrary, is Christ-like, humble, a servant of all, desiring to give all glory and honor to God the Father in heaven.

Time for God differs from time for humans. God created time, but He is not bound by time or space. Because God is eternal, His understanding of time is far beyond human comprehension. "[W]ith the Lord one day is as a thousand years, and a thousand years as one day" (2 Peter 3:8) offers a conceptualization of time that baffles the mind. Humans understand a day to mean twenty-four hours and a thousand years to be 365,000 days or 8,760,000 hours. Peter warns us that the way "some count" is not the way God counts. God waits patiently, "not wishing that any should perish, but that all reach repentance" (2 Peter 3:9). Read carefully. God does not want anyone to suffer eternal damnation. However, God gives free will to everyone. Jesus speaks very clearly that those who choose to reject divine mercy will receive eternal punishment (Matthew 25:46).

Believers must live lives of holiness awaiting the Day of the Lord. For, "according to his promise we wait for new heavens and a new earth in which righteousness dwells" (2 Peter 3:13). Peter encourages the Christians to be zealous, to grow in grace and to be found without spot or blemish. Studying God's Word demonstrates that you are striving to grow in holiness and grace!

> Through the gospel message, the Church offers a force for liberation which promotes development precisely because it leads to conversion of heart and of ways of thinking, fosters the recognition of each person's dignity, encourages solidarity, commitment and service of one's neighbor, and gives everyone a place in God's plan, which is the building of his kingdom of peace and justice, beginning already in this life. This is the biblical perspective of the "new heavens and a new earth" (cf. Isaiah 65:17, 2 Peter 3:13, Revelation 21:1), which has been the stimulus and goal of mankind's advancement in history. Man's development derives from God, and from the model of Jesus—God and man—and must lead back to God.
> Pope John Paul II, *Redemptoris Missio*, (December 7, 1990) no. 59.1.

1. To whom is this letter addressed?   2 Peter 1:1

2. How can you share (partake) in the divine nature?   2 Peter 1:3-4   *CCC 1129*

3. Where does justification come from? Define this term.   *CCC 1996*

4. What must you do to grow in holiness?   2 Peter 1:5-7

Make every effort to supplement your faith with

5. Compare the following passages for other advice in growing in virtue.

Romans 5:3-4	*Galatians 5:16, 18, 22*	*James 1:2-5*

6. Explain 2 Peter 1:13-15 in your own words.

7. Compare the following passages.

Matthew 17:1-8	2 Peter 1:16-18

8. Describe the imagery in 2 Peter 1:19.

9. What can you learn about the importance of Scripture and Tradition from the Bible?

Psalm 119:105	
2 Thessalonians 2:15	
2 Timothy 3:14-17	
2 Peter 1:20-21	

10. List some ways to identify false teachers.   2 Peter 2:1-3, 10-22. Jude 16, 18, 19

11. What did God do to the angels and people of old who sinned?   2 Peter 2:4-8, Jude 6

12. Describe the Lord's Coming *(The Day of the Lord).*

Joel 2:28-32	
Amos 5:18-20	
Matthew 24:42-44	
2 Peter 3:10	

13. Does God desire anyone to perish?

Ezekiel 18:23	
2 Peter 3:9	
CCC 1037	

14. Define "Hell." ***CCC 1033***

15. What would you say to someone who doesn't believe in hell? ***CCC 1034, 1035***

16. Does Jesus have anything to say about hell?

Matthew 5:22	
Matthew 5:29	
Matthew 10:28	
Matthew 13:40-42	
Matthew 13:49-50	

17. For what do Christians hope?

Isaiah 65:17, 66:22	
2 Peter 3:13	
Revelation 21:1-27	

18. What pledge do Catholics have of this hope in "new heavens and new earth?" ***CCC 1405***

19. Describe "Christ's reign in power and glory." ***CCC 671***

20. What closing admonitions are given in 2 Peter 3:14-18?

21. List one practical thing you could do to prepare yourself for the Day of the Lord.

JOEL
Prophet of the Spirit

Memory Verse

**"And it shall come to pass afterward,
that I will pour out my spirit on all flesh;
your sons and your daughters shall prophesy,
your old men shall dream dreams,
and your young men shall see visions.
Even upon the menservants and maidservants
in those days, I will pour out my spirit"**

JOEL 2:28-29

Meet Joel. *Yo-El* is an excellent and beautiful Hebrew name, that combines the divine name *Yo* (short for YHWH) with the divine title *"El"* (the basic term for God). Hence the name means, "The Lord is God." The name Elijah contains the two terms simply reversed: *Eli-Yah* (My God is the Lord). These two terms occur next to each other many times in the Old and even in the New Testament, as in Thomas' profession of faith, "My Lord and my God." (John 20:28). Once in the Psalter there appears the simple statement, "(Know that) the LORD is God" (Psalm 100:3). A more simple profession of faith than that is hardly possible, except for the equivalent New Testament statement, "Jesus Christ is Lord" (Philippians 2:11).

It is not surprising, then, that twelve individuals bear the name *Yo-El* in the pages of the Old Testament. We know nothing about the biography of the late, post-exilic prophet Joel, other than the mention of his father's name, Pethuel. Joel himself seems to have been advanced in years at the time he received his oracles, since the second verse reads: "Hear this, you aged men." Joel speaks about young people later in his book, but he seems to identify first with the older generation.

Joel and the Locusts ~ During Joel's lifetime a plague of locusts had invaded the land (Joel 1:2 to 2:27), so great that no one living could remember a worse catastrophe. Locust plague strips the land of all vegetation and leaves people and animals to starve in their wake: "It has laid waste my vines, and splintered my fig trees; it has stripped off their bark and thrown it down; their branches are made white" (Joel 1:7).

Sheep have sharper teeth than cattle and can graze in fields even after cattle have eaten everything they could. Sheep can even do damage to a pasture if they over-graze. The locusts have left nothing even for the sheep. Joel's eye-witness descriptions show real understanding of nature and of agriculture: "The herds of cattle are perplexed because there is no pasture for them; even the flocks of sheep are dismayed" (Joel 1:18).

One disaster follows another, as a normally healthy ecosystem collapses: "What the cutting locust left, the swarming locust has eaten. What the swarming locust left, the hopping locust has eaten, and what the hopping locust left, the destroying locust has eaten" (Joel 1:4).

In the days of Moses, the plague of locusts was the eighth of the ten plagues (Exodus 10:1-20), more terrible than foul water, frogs, gnats, flies, cattle plague, boils or hail. Only utter darkness and the death of the firstborn cast more fear into the hearts of the Egyptians than the plague of locusts. Since the locust plague signified coming liberation for the Israelites in Egypt, the locust plague in Judea seven hundred years later signified to Joel only temporary disaster but eventual blessing.

The liturgical act of mourning the locusts seems critical in Yo-El's thinking;
the ritual of Israel acts as a catalyst to bring about the divine blessing:
— "The priests mourn, the ministers of the LORD" (Joel 1:9).
— "Gird on sackcloth and lament, O priests; wail, O ministers of the altar.
Go in, pass the night in sackcloth, O ministers of my God" (Joel 1:13).
— "Between the vestibule and the altar let the priests, the ministers of the LORD, weep"
(Joel 2:17).

The phrase "between the vestibule and the altar" describes the court of the priests, which only men of the tribe of Levi could enter to recite the psalms and perform the acts of sacrifice. Joel seems to have personal familiarity with this courtyard and so could very well have been a member of the tribe of Levi himself, as was Moses before him.

A variety of horns marked different celebrations in the Jewish liturgical year:

- Trumpets ~ "On the day of your gladness also, and at your appointed feasts, and at the beginnings of your months, you shall blow the trumpets over your burnt offerings and over the sacrifices of your peace offerings" (Numbers 10:10).

- Ram's Horn ~ On Rosh Hashanah, the first day of the first month of the New Year, the ram's horn was blown, since God had given a ram for Abraham to sacrifice in place of his son Isaac (Genesis 22:13). The sound of the ram horn reminded the people of Israel that God had spared them for another year in his service.

The trumpets in Joel (Joel 2:1 and 15), in Hosea (5:8), in Amos (3:6) and in Zephaniah (1:16) signify not the New Year but the approach of danger and of the great day of the Lord: "[W]hen you go to war in your land against the adversary who oppresses you, then you shall sound an alarm with the trumpets, that you may be remembered before the LORD your God" (Numbers 10:9).

This kind of trumpet will sound the alarm on the great Last Day: "[W]e shall all be changed, in a moment, in the twinkling of an eye, at the last trumpet. For the trumpet will sound, and the dead will be raised imperishable, and we shall be changed" (1 Corinthians 15:51-52).

The final plagues of the Book of Revelation are each accompanied by a trumpet: "Now the seven angels who had the seven trumpets made ready to blow them" (Revelation 8:6). The fifth angel's trumpet will call forth a plague of locusts, with a scorpion's sting and appearance like a warhorse (Revelation 9:1-11). We can see how the connection between trumpets and locusts, which originated in the book of Joel, continues and is developed yet further in Revelation.

Jews, Christians and Moslems all believe in the Final Judgment, which Joel is one of the first to describe: "The day of the Lord is coming, it is near, a day of darkness and gloom, a day of clouds and thick darkness!" (Joel 2:1-2). The final four events for every human being in all of human history are death, judgment, heaven and hell. Each of us, man or woman, king or slave, rich or poor, will experience death, judgment, and ultimately either heaven or hell.

<table>
<tr><td>

And just as it is appointed for men to die once, and after that comes judgment, so Christ, having been offered once to bear the sins of many, will appear a second time, not to deal with sin but to save those who are eagerly waiting for him.

Hebrews 9:27-28

</td><td>

Do not rejoice in temporal successes, for you certainly do not know that they will assure you eternal life. At the evening of life, you will be judged on your love. Oh, how blessed are they who shall enjoy the vision of the Most Holy Trinity.

St. John of the Cross
(1542-1592 AD)
Dichos 64, 59, 181.

</td></tr>
</table>

Following the particular judgment of each person, there will also be the judgment of the Last Day, when the conduct of each person and the secrets of hearts will be brought into the light. On this Judgment Day, Jesus will proclaim: "Truly, I say to you, as you did it to one of the least of these my brothers, you did it to me" (Matthew 25:40).

Outpouring of Prophecy ~ Halfway through the Book of Joel, in the middle of the second chapter, the priests recite the following liturgical prayer: "Spare thy people, O LORD, and make not thy heritage a reproach, a byword among the nations. Why should they say among the peoples, 'Where is their God?'" (Joel 2:17)

This prayer has a powerful logic. We do not ask to be rescued by God because of our merits, but because we bear His Name, which is worthy of all praise. Our salvation is to God's glory. As the Psalmist says, "Not to us, O LORD, not to us, but to thy name give glory" (Psalm 115:1). The prayer of the priests in Joel even contains a quotation from this same Psalm: "Why should the nations say, 'Where is their God?' Our God is in the heavens; he does whatever he pleases" (Psalm 115:2-3; see also Psalm 42:3, 10).

When a narrative passage contains a small poetic quotation, we are to understand that they recited the entire poem on that occasion. Hence, we should visualize Joel's priests reciting all of Psalm 115, which forms part of the Great Hallel of Passover:

Psalm 115

Not to us, O LORD, not to us, but to thy name give glory,
for the sake of thy steadfast love and thy faithfulness!
Why should the nations say, 'Where is their God?'
Our God is in the heavens;
he does whatever he pleases.
Their idols are silver and gold, the work of men's hands.
They have mouths, but do not speak; eyes, but do not see.
They have ears, but do not hear; noses, but do not smell.
They have hands, but do not feel; feet, but do not walk;
and they do not make a sound in their throat.
Those who make them are like them; so are all who trust in them.

O Israel, trust in the LORD!
He is their help and their shield.
O house of Aaron, put your trust in the LORD!
He is their help and their shield.
You who fear the LORD, trust in the LORD!
He is their help and their shield.
The LORD has been mindful of us, and He will bless us;
he will bless the house of Israel;
he will bless the house of Aaron;
he will bless those who fear the LORD, both small and great.

May the LORD give you increase, you and your children!
May you be blessed by the LORD, who made heaven and earth!
The heavens are the LORD's heavens,
but the earth he has given to the sons of men.
The dead do not praise the LORD, nor do any that go down into silence.
But we will bless the LORD from this time forth and for evermore.
Praise the LORD!

Notice that this psalm contains both a strong profession of monotheistic faith, renouncing the false gods of the nations, and a benediction pronounced upon the whole people of God. This is clearly a priestly prayer, for the Levitical priesthood was entrusted with the responsibility of blessing the people in the name of the Lord.

The pronouncement of this blessing from Psalm 115 has even more effect in the prophecy of Joel than the sounding of the trumpets. It is the priestly blessing, not the ritual trumpet, that ushers in a whole different mood from the midpoint onward: "Then the LORD became jealous for his land, and had pity on his people" (Joel 2:18).

Now there is enough grain, wine and oil. Now the invader from the north is cast away into the desert and into the sea. Now the rains come and the harvests overflow. Now the Lord's own spirit is poured out upon all flesh, so that the young and the old, men and women shall have the gift of prophecy.

It seems that Joel understands this outpouring to take place only upon the nation of Israel, but the grammar of the passage does not contain this limitation. It clearly says, "all flesh," not "all Israelite flesh" (Joel 2:28). So St. Peter is fully justified on the first Pentecost Sunday when he announces that this prophecy includes all nations (Acts 2:17). *Clearly the outpouring of the Holy Spirit is the greatest moment in the Book of Joel, and the descent of the Holy Spirit upon the apostles is the perfect fulfillment of this prophecy.*

The rest of the Book of Joel seems an afterthought, but actually it contains another valuable vision of the great final judgment, which will take place at the end of time. Joel describes a reversal of Isaiah's vision of final peace. Where Isaiah and Micah prophesy that swords will be beat into plowshares, Joel prophesies the reverse, that plowshares will be beat into swords (Joel 3:10). This is not really a contradiction. Joel refers to the great final battle (Armageddon), while Isaiah speaks of the final peace that will follow.

Again, the apocalyptic vision of Joel's third chapter seems less wonderful than the outpouring of the Spirit in Joel's second chapter. We place our hopes more on the operation of the Holy Spirit in our lives than in great battles, final or otherwise.

The peace for which we hope is already in our hearts as a gift of that Spirit,

so that we do not have to await an apocalyptic peace in the future.

The power of God poured out on Pentecost is greater than all armies of this time

or of all times put together, including those of the final age.

Through the fulfillment of Joel's vision, we have the power, and we have the peace.

At no time should we forget that the Holy Spirit inspired Psalm 115, and that powerful prayer will always act as a miraculous key to unlock the potential for peace in our hearts. Just as it inspired Joel, it can still inspire us.

1. Read The Book of Joel and write your favorite verse.

2. To whom is Joel speaking in Joel 1:1-7, and what is he describing?

3. Compare the following passages.

Exodus 10:12-20
Joel 1:4
Revelation 9:1-10

4. What directives are given in Joel 1:8 and Joel 1:11?

5. List two practical instructions given in Joel 1:13-14.

6. Find the common spiritual activity called for in the following passages.

Judges 20:26	
Jeremiah 36:6, 9	
Matthew 4:2	
Acts 13:2-3	

7. What is foretold in Joel 1:15? What is coming?

8. Why is the horn blown?

Hosea 5:8-9	
Joel 2:1-2	
Amos 3:6-8	
Zephaniah 1:16	
Revelation 8:6-13	

9. What natural disasters are foretold in Joel 2:10?

10. What does the Lord request?   Joel 2:12-13

11. Describe the Lord from the following passages.

Exodus 34:6	
Nehemiah 9:31	
Psalm 86:15	
Joel 2:13	

12. What hope is described in Joel 2:14?

13. What activities are called for in Joel 2:15-17?

14. Joel describes times of chastisement followed by times of blessings. Can you identify parallel times of trial followed by times of blessing in your own personal life? List some of them.

15. What three things can you do to express interior penance to God? *CCC 1434*

<table>
<tr><td></td></tr>
<tr><td></td></tr>
<tr><td></td></tr>
</table>

16. What does the Church offer each year for your spiritual purification? *CCC 1438*

CCC 1438

17. What promise can you find in Joel 2:28-29 RSV or Joel 3:1-2 NAB?

18. What promise is given in John 14:16-17, 26?

19. How and when are these promises fulfilled?   Acts 2:1-4

20. Which New Testament apostle explains the fulfillment of the prophet Joel? Acts 2:14-21.

21. When does the Christian expect the fulfillment of this promise? *CCC 1302*

22. What effects can you expect?   *CCC 1303*

From this fact, ____

____.   *CCC 1303*

23. If you would like to receive a greater outpouring of the Holy Spirit, pray this prayer.

O Holy Spirit, Beloved of my soul, I adore You.
Enlighten, Guide, Strengthen and Console me;
Tell me what to say and do and command me to do it.
I promise to be submissive in all things, only show me what is Your Will.

1 & 2 TIMOTHY, TITUS
Pastoral Wisdom

Memory Verse

**"All scripture is inspired by God and profitable
for teaching, for reproof, for correction, and for training in righteousness,
that the man of God may be complete,
equipped for every good work."**

2 TIMOTHY 3:16-17

Three small books cluster near the end of the Bible, providing great pastoral wisdom for believers. 1 and 2 Timothy and Titus are called the "pastoral epistles" because they speak specifically to the shepherds of the Church and provide practical wisdom for dealing with Church discipline, refuting heretics and bringing order into the Church. Although authorship can be debated, assume that these letters are written by the apostle Paul. These books see the Church as the source of truth (1 Timothy 3:15) and the household in which believers live and thrive (2 Timothy 2:20). The Church safeguards the good news of the Gospel, the deposit of faith, a fixed body of doctrine.

God brings order out of chaos and Christians respect the order provided by God in creation, in the home, and in the Church. The Church, the household of faith meets the challenges of the house churches in early Christianity. New Testament domestic codes promote order and virtue, showing pagans that Christians strive for peace and godliness. Practical wisdom strengthens the bonds within the family, the basic unit of the Church, and the Christian community as a whole. The household in New Testament times involved extended families, slaves and tenant workers. While the Bible never promotes slavery as a good, it provides practical wisdom and hope for people who find themselves subjected to living in that difficult situation.

The First Letter of Paul to Timothy opposes false teaching and gives practical guidance for problems in church administration. Heretics divide the Christian community. While the exact nature of the heresy cannot be conclusively determined from the text, there are references to myths, genealogies and vain discussions of the law.

Paul identifies himself as a servant of Jesus Christ and a model for sinners. Paul acknowledges his sin and testifies to the mercy of God found in Christ Jesus, who came into the world to save sinners. Paul, foremost of sinners, who has received mercy and grace, becomes an example for other sinners in need of salvation. Jesus came into the world to save sinners, and Paul never tires of promoting this good news for the honor and glory of God.

Timothy, commissioned by the laying on of hands (1 Timothy 4:14) receives encouragement from Paul to carry on the good work. Paul commends Timothy's filial obedience and strengthens him for the fight ahead. Paul also warns Timothy of the consequences that can result from failing to be steadfast in fulfilling his obligations. The special relationship which Paul and Timothy share is evident by his affectionate address "Timothy, my son" (1 Timothy 1:18). Paul seems to be passing the baton to Timothy and encouraging him to continue to do the same. Vocations thrive; the Church continues.

Communal prayer in the liturgical celebrations concerns itself with the needs of all. One can only imagine what might have been going on during worship in the early Church to warrant such admonitions. Nonetheless, proper conduct and order are demanded. Men are to pray fervently without anger or quarreling. Women are encouraged to display modesty and clothe themselves in good deeds. The role of preaching, teaching and authority falls on men. Perhaps Paul envisioned the contemporary dangers inherent in seeing religion as something for women and children. In many Church settings today, you might look around and wonder where all the men have gone.

"Yet woman will be saved through bearing children, if she continues in faith and love and holiness, with modesty" (1 Timothy 2:15) is a puzzling verse which has been widely debated. It may connote that the woman will be saved through the birth of the Child, Jesus Christ. Or, the verse may suggest that the woman will be brought safely through childbirth. Another possibility is that mothers who bring forth children in faith and love will experience salvation in Christ.

Relationships are of utmost importance in the family and in the Church. Bishops and deacons must be of exemplary character, similar to good heads of households. They must be sensible, temperate, hospitable and desire to serve the people and lead worship. Right conduct is prescribed for men and women, the old and the young, widows, presbyters and slaves.

Some of the common sayings prevalent in our society, even among non-churchgoing people find their origin in this pastoral letter.

- We brought nothing into the world, and we cannot take anything out of the world. 1 Timothy 6:7
- If we have food and clothing, with these we shall be content with that. 1 Timothy 6:8
- For the love of money is the root of all evils!   1 Timothy 6:10

Believers are warned not to love money, for greed causes some to wander away from the faith and plunge themselves into ruin and destruction. However, the wealthy are encouraged here to use their riches to perform good works, to be kind and generous, thus laying up for themselves a treasure in heaven. Wealth can be used to build up the body of Christ, to alleviate hunger and suffering and to advance the spread of the Gospel. Indeed the generosity of Christians throughout the centuries has built hospitals, schools, orphanages, churches, and supported missionary activities.

The Second Letter to Timothy seems to have been written at the close of Paul's life. "For I am already on the point of being sacrificed; the time of my departure has come. I have fought the good fight, I have finished the race, I have kept the faith" (2 Timothy 4:6-7). Paul, aware that his death is imminent, bequeaths his last will and testament to his beloved disciple, Timothy. Paul chronicles the transmission of faith from Timothy's grandmother, to his mother, to him. A goal and longing for all Christians is to pass on the fullness of faith to the next generation, our children. Paul encourages Timothy to rekindle the gift of God received through the laying on of hands, when he received the grace and power and anointing of the Holy Spirit for service to the Church.

Paul, well-acquainted with suffering, offers the benefit of his suffering for others. Paul unites his suffering with the Passion of Christ, interceding for the salvation of souls. Religious sisters often told school children "to offer it up" when experiencing some hardship. This encouragement can be found in Paul's admonition to Timothy: "Share in suffering as a good soldier of Christ Jesus" (2 Timothy 2:3). One of the treasures of the Catholic Church is the understanding of redemptive suffering. Pain and sorrows come to all human beings. When suffering comes your way, you have a choice. You can fight suffering with bitterness, anger and denial, or you can embrace suffering and offer it to Christ to be used in a way pleasing to Him in effecting some good for some other soul.

The apostle issues more warnings against false teachings, profane and idle talk. Quarreling must be avoided. Stay away from senseless controversies. Rather, correct the erring brothers with gentleness, hoping that God will grant them the grace to repent and come to know the truth and escape from the snare of the devil. The Christian must hold fast to sound doctrine, be obedient to those that Christ has set in authority, and practice virtue.

Interestingly, 2 Timothy 3:16 is the first passage in the Bible that speaks of the divine inspiration of the Old Testament. The Bible, as you know it, hasn't been completed or compiled when this letter is being penned. Paul's love for Sacred Scripture is evident when he proclaims: "All scripture is inspired by God and profitable for teaching, for reproof, for correction, and for training in righteousness, that the man of God may be complete, equipped for every good work" (2 Timothy 3:16-17). Clearly, Timothy had been given a love of God's Word from his mother and grandmother and from his spiritual father in the faith. The effort that you exert right now in reading and studying God's Word enables you to be equipped for every good work and to share God's Word with others.

At the end of his life, Paul asks for his cloak, his books, and above all the parchments to be brought to him (2 Timothy 4:13). What wonderful example to be reading the Word of God at the twilight of one's life! St. Thomas Aquinas said, "The closer Paul was to death, the stronger he felt the need of the Scriptures." And, St. John Chrysostom, (344-407 AD) calls Paul's letter a "testament of consolation" in which Paul uses words to describe his death that are conducive to consolation and joy so that death is seen as a pilgrimage or even a transfer to a better world.

The Letter to Titus presupposes the Church as an essential, vital, thriving institution in the world. The earlier First Letter to Timothy presents the Church as "the household of God, which is the church of the living God, the bulwark of the truth" (1 Timothy 3:15). The body of Christ is seen as a family, headed by the bishop who guides and protects the deposit of faith. Sound doctrine can be found in the authoritative teaching of the Church.

Some people insist that all they need is the Bible alone. However, the Bible doesn't say that! Thousands of different denominations all claiming to have found the truth based on the Bible alone prove the inadequacy of such a premise. In fact, these pastoral letters underscore the importance of the Church and the Magisterium to guide the believer into the fullness of truth and promote sound doctrine. St. Paul says, "[H]e called you through our gospel, so that you may obtain the glory of our Lord Jesus Christ. So then, brethren, stand firm and hold to the traditions which you were taught by us, either by word of mouth or by letter" (2 Thessalonians 2:14-15).

Jesus came and built Himself a Church, and the Bible came several generations later. Jesus said, "And I tell you, you are Peter, and on this rock I will build my Church, and the powers of death shall not prevail against it" (Matthew 16:18). Catholics finds great consolation in knowing that in areas where the Bible is silent (e.g. gambling, artificial insemination, cloning), the pope and bishops in union with him provide clear, sound teaching.

The Church always returns to the example of Jesus Christ to determine norms for upright living. Even though people in the Church sin, and leaders may fail and show poor example, Christ never sinned. Hence, we look to the perfect example of our Lord Jesus Christ. Moreover, when lay people, priests or bishops sin, the mercy of God is always available to the repentant sinner in the Sacrament of Reconciliation, despite the severity of the offense against God.

Titus offers two beautiful Christological passages, which the Church offers in the readings for Mass on Christmas. Titus 2:11-14 is read at midnight Mass on Christmas Eve, and Titus 3:3-6 is read in the second reading for the Mass at dawn on Christmas Day. Perhaps these passages, handed down by the apostle in fulfillment of the Old Testament prophets' hopes, would provide rich food for quiet reflection and meditation here.

> **For the grace of God has appeared**
> **for the salvation of all men,**
> **training us to renounce irreligion and worldly passions,**
> **and to live sober, upright, and godly lives in this world,**
> **awaiting our blessed hope,**
> **the appearing of the glory of our great God and Savior Jesus Christ,**
> **who gave himself for us**
> **to redeem us from all iniquity**
> **and to purify for himself a people of his own who are zealous for good deeds.**
> TITUS 2:11-14

"[B]ut when the goodness and loving kindness of God our Savior appeared,
he saved us,
not because of deeds done by us in righteousness,
but in virtue of his own mercy,
by the washing of regeneration and renewal in the Holy Spirit,
which he poured upon us richly through Jesus Christ our Savior,
so that we might be justified by his grace
and become heirs in hope of eternal life."

TITUS 3:4-7

1. Read the First Letter to Timothy and write your favorite verse below.

2. Write down what you can learn about Timothy from the following passages.

1 Timothy 1:1-3	
1 Timothy 1:18	
2 Timothy 1:1-5	
2 Timothy 1:6	
2 Timothy 2:2	

3. How should prayer and worship be conducted? 1 Timothy 2:1-12

4. Describe as many characteristics of bishops as you can from 1 Timothy 3:1-7.

5. What is the mystery of our religion?   1 Timothy 3:14-16

6. Tell everything you can about the Church from 1 Timothy 3:15. Where do you find
    "the Church?"

7. What problems occur in 1 Timothy 4:1-5?

8. List some specific instructions Paul gives to the Timothy in the following verses.

1 Timothy 4:11	
1 Timothy 4:12	
1 Timothy 4:13	
1 Timothy 4:14-15	

9. Provide some practical direction for dealing with the following people. Give verses.

An Older Man	
Younger Men	
Older Women	
Younger Women	
Widows	
Slaves	

10. Offer as much wisdom as you can find on the proper use of wealth from 1 Timothy 6:3-19.

11. Write the verse from 1 Timothy 6 that most challenges your personal use of money.

12. Read 2 Timothy and write your favorite verse from this book.

13. What kind of spirit did God give us and what does He expect of us?   2 Timothy 1:7, 9

14. What did God accomplish through Jesus for us?   2 Timothy 1:9-10

15. According to 2 Timothy 1:11 what three roles was Paul appointed to for the Gospel?

_____________________   _____________________   _____________________

16. Explain the analogies that Paul makes from the following examples in 2 Timothy 2.

Soldier
Athlete
Farmer

17. With which of the above can you most identify?

18. Salvation in Jesus Christ with its eternal glory is described by Paul in 2 Timothy 2:11-13.

If we have died with Him ...	*we shall also*
If we	

19. What positive thing can you learn about Timothy's family life from 2 Timothy 3:14-15.

20. Can you share a practical way in which this Bible study has helped you? 2 Timothy 3:16-17

21. Read the Letter to Titus and write your favorite verse.

22. Use one word to describe the behavior in Titus 1:16.

23. What is commanded in Titus 2:1?

24. What admonitions are given to the following groups of people in 2 Timothy 2?

Older Men	
Older Women	
Young Women	
Young Men	
Slaves	

25. Write one piece of practical advice from Titus 3 that could be applied to your life.

ZEPHANIAH & MALACHI
Prophets of Doom and Hope

Memory Verse

**"For the LORD their God
will be mindful of them and restore their fortunes."**

ZEPHANIAH 2:7

Meet Zephaniah. Apart from verse 1, we know absolutely nothing about the biography of prophet Zephaniah. Nonetheless, in its coded way, this little genealogy tells us a great deal about the man: "Zephaniah the son of Cushi, son of Gedaliah, son of Amariah, son of Hezekiah, in the days of Josiah the son of Amon, king of Judah" (Zephaniah 1:1).

By tracing the ancestry of Zephaniah back to the fifth generation, this verse seeks to connect the prophet with Hezekiah, King of Judah in the days of Isaiah and Micah. The name Hezekiah is not very common, and it is unlikely than any other Hezekiah was significant enough to merit such interest. If I said, "I am the great-great-grandson of Lincoln," every American would assume that I meant the Civil War president, even though other people have been named Lincoln. So the opening verse declares our prophet to be of royal blood and descended in the direct line from one of the kings of Judah. That could explain why he can get away with making such violent prophecies. Perhaps only a scion of the royal family would have been able to say such things with impunity. When prophets who came from the lower classes tried doing so, they were frequently rebuffed.

King Josiah, who reigned in the time of Zephaniah, seems to have heeded his distant cousin's message, because he restored the life of the nation to better accord with the law of the Lord. His efforts had limited success, and when he died in battle, it was a terrible blow from which the Judean state never really recovered. Zephaniah was recognized as a true prophet, and his book accepted into the Bible because his prophecies of doom came true, probably within his own lifetime.

Day of Wrath ~ Biblical prophecy is both specific and general, both timely and timeless. Zephaniah speaks of a day of doom close at hand: "The great day of the LORD is near, near and hastening fast" (Zephaniah 1:14). Nonetheless, his description also points forward to the end times, to the great Last Day: "I will utterly sweep away everything from the face of the earth," (1:2).

Zephaniah's poetry is so powerful that it has had a major impact on art and literature: "A day of wrath is that day, a day of distress and anguish, a day of ruin and devastation, a day of darkness and gloom, a day of clouds and thick darkness" (Zephaniah 1:15). One thinks of Michelangelo's great painting, "The Last Judgment" in the Sistine Chapel. One also thinks of the famous medieval sequence used in the funeral liturgy.

Dies Irae, dies illa *solvit saeclum in favilla* *teste David cum Sibylla*	**A day of wrath, that day** **will dissolve the world in ashes,** **as David testifies, with the Sibyll.**

For seven centuries this sequence was sung in the Roman Funeral Liturgy, for popes and sinners, for paupers and kings. During the most recent liturgical renewal, it disappeared from the ritual, as the liturgical color changed from black to white. We used to place a black pall over the casket (whence the saying, "casting a pall over something"), but now we use a white one. Our emphasis has changed from the fear of judgment to the hope of resurrection.

Since people are grieving anyway over the death of their loved one, perhaps that is not the moment for us to use Zephaniah's imagery. After all, Jesus said, "Blessed are the merciful, for they shall obtain mercy" (Matthew 5:7). So we should be merciful on those who are in the midst of their worst griefs, not to quote Zephaniah's poetry at that moment. The right time to talk about the four last things—Death and Judgment, Heaven and Hell—is not at the funeral but while the patient is still alive and can do something about it.

It would be a false mercy to deprive people of hearing about the final judgment, because it is not just Zephaniah's message, but the Lord's. Jesus Himself, the Word of God incarnate, incorporates the last judgment into His preaching. Without God's final judicial correction, all the misfeasance of human judgment would go uncorrected. In the end, the innocent who have been falsely accused and punished, even executed, will receive vindication, and the guilty who escaped scot-free will face justice. Those who have committed vast crimes against humanity will stand before a truly competent tribunal. Without the last day, we have nothing but an all-too-human system of justice, imperfect indeed. In fact, we might go so far as to say that without God's Tribunal, there is no such thing as real justice, for only God knows the thoughts and motives of the heart, in which true guilt and innocence reside. Final justice remains an indispensable part of our Creed, as we recite every Sunday together: "He will come again in glory to judge the living and the dead."

Survival of a remnant ~ After more than two chapters of relentless pessimism, Zephaniah's message turns upward towards the end: "I will leave in the midst of you a people humble and lowly. They shall seek refuge in the name of the LORD, those who are left in Israel; they shall do no wrong and utter no lies, nor shall there be found in their mouth a deceitful tongue" (Zephaniah 3:12-13). These are the *Anawim*, the poor of the Lord, in whom lived the hopes and yearnings for the coming of the Messiah. Such as these were Zachary and Elizabeth, Joseph and Mary, and into their midst was born the Savior. Luke highly praises Simeon in these words: "[T]his man was righteous and devout, looking for the consolation of Israel, and the Holy Spirit was upon him" (Luke 2:25). Any nation with such holy souls nestled within it shall not be put to shame.

The Old Testament prophets taught that a remnant would survive the destruction of the nation, and the Lord's favor would rest upon this remnant. The promises to Israel would be fulfilled in them and in their Offspring for ever. In his book of violent images, Zephaniah contrasts the disaster to many with the favor to a remnant few. His disaster imagery has made more of an impact than his remnant imagery at the end, but neither set of images would be complete without the other.

Zephaniah looked straight and unblinkingly at the worst things upon the earth—war, ruin, and total annihilation of life in the universe. Yet he emerges with a message of hope. What kind of hope can console a vision of such universal catastrophe? Only a hope of even more cosmic significance: "I will remove disaster from you, so that you will not bear reproach for

it" (Zephaniah 3:18). This cannot be a mere historical solution to a metaphysical disaster, otherwise the consolation of the book's finale fails to rise to the necessity created by the body of the work. What kind of disaster will God remove? None other than the worst disaster— the death of body and soul. Only salvation from sin and death can solve the horrors of this world. Amazingly, after all his knee-knocking visions, Zephaniah can say: "Do not fear, O Zion; let not your hands grow weak. The LORD, your God is in your midst, a warrior who gives victory" (Zephaniah 3:17). The presence of the Incarnate Son of God in the Holy Family in Bethlehem, Egypt, Nazareth, and Jerusalem, in our churches, our homes and our hearts is the fulfillment, and the only adequate fulfillment, of this prophecy.

Meet Malachi. The prophet Malachi is never mentioned outside his little book itself. Nonetheless, from internal evidence, we can learn something about his background. He seems to have been a prophet in the southern Kingdom of Judah, after the fall of the northern kingdom. He thus lived between two disasters, a time when it was difficult to be optimistic. The southern kingdom had depended heavily upon the economy of the north. At the time the northern kingdom fell, the Assyrians attacked the south and shattered its rural economy. In Malachi's time there was a general poverty, which explains why animals that were not spotless were being sacrificed in the temple. Few animals had unspotted fur, and were not "lame or sick" (Malachi 1:8).

Malachi must have been a contemporary of Jeremiah, who suffered persecution for speaking boldly in the name of the Lord. We do not know anything about the relationship between the two of them, whether they belonged to the same prophetic school or not. Their books do not have much in common other than the same general background canvas.

Malachi's message ~ The Lord is King! In the first chapter of the Book of Malachi, the Lord proclaims: "For I am a great King, says the LORD of hosts, and my Name is feared among the nations" (Malachi 1:14). "Melek," the Hebrew word for king, sounds very similar to Malachi. The name Malachi comes from a different root, but they are similar enough for a kind of word-play here.

When the Lord says that He is a great King, He means not just simply great, and not just very great, but absolutely the greatest. The King of Jerusalem was a little king, and the King of Egypt a big one, but the Lord God is King on a different and much higher level. What is happening in this verse is that the Lord is borrowing language from human politics to explain His own divinity. It was common biblical practice to borrow vocabulary from other fields and apply it to God, by analogy. Just as the king ruled in Jerusalem, the Lord ruled in heaven; that is the general idea.

Some of the psalms speak of God as enthroning the king, and others speak of God as if He were Himself king. One of the psalms puts it in question-and-answer form: "Who is this King of glory? The LORD of hosts, he is the King of glory!" (Psalm 24:10).

One of the important teachings of the Bible is the absolute supremacy of God. No person or nation can exist without Him, and no ruler can remain in power without God allowing it. All temporal power is secondary and derived, while only God's power is eternal and infinite. There is no absolute monarch other than God alone. Of course, human beings like to exalt themselves and seek adulation. Because nature hates a vacuum, nations that are officially atheistic seem to be the first to promote the state itself as an object of worship. The Bible allows no cult of personality.

St. Peter states it succinctly: "Fear God. Honor the emperor" (1 Peter 2:17). This doesn't look very revolutionary on the face of it. The statement seems to say we should accept the government of God and the current political arrangement, whatever it may be. Look a little deeper, however, and you find a profound revolutionary sentiment. In Peter's time, the emperor claimed to be a god! When Peter and others refused to worship him, they paid for it with their lives! If Peter were not a true revolutionary, then why was he killed?

The fact remains that from the time of the Maccabees on to the twenty-first century, millions of Jews and Christians have yielded their lives rather than give to human rulers the worship that belongs to God alone. This passive but massive resistance to overarching government has been the principal factor influencing the democratization of political life in the Western World. It was not atheists or secularists who defanged the state by withholding false worship from it, but rather believers in the supremacy of the One, True God.

Remember that Peter is the one to whom Christ said, "Render therefore to Caesar the things that are Caesar's, and to God the things that are God's." This statement was so important that three of the four evangelists report it (Matthew 22:21, Mark 12:17 and Luke 20:25). Peter learned this lesson well from the hands of Christ Himself, who in turn drew upon the language of the prophets.

Malachi the messenger ~ The third chapter of Malachi begins with a very important prophecy. "Behold, I send my messenger to prepare the way before me, and the Lord whom you seek will suddenly come to his temple" (Malachi 3:1). In Hebrew, the name Malachi means "my messenger." So this verse could be translated "Behold, I send Malachi to prepare the way before me." Both translations are valid in a certain sense. The immediate messenger whom the Lord sent was Malachi himself, whose name means "My Messenger." Eventually, however, there will be another messenger, who will come immediately before the Lord Himself.

Jesus quotes this passage from Malachi when He speaks about John the Baptist. "This is he of whom it is written, 'Behold I send my messenger before thy face, who shall prepare thy way before thee. Truly, I say to you, among those born of women there has risen no one greater than John the Baptist; yet he who is least in the kingdom of heaven is greater than he'" (Matthew 11:10-11).

Though Matthew does not report that Jesus quoted the second half of the verse, He may have actually done so. Even if He did not, both He and His listeners doubtless knew the passage well: "I send my messenger … and the Lord whom you seek will suddenly come." The coming of John fulfills the first half of the prophecy, but the coming of Jesus fulfills the rest. Anyone less than Jesus would not match the prophecies of Malachi any more than those of Zephaniah. The coming of a mere human ruler would not have realized the requirements of prophecy.

This is the message of Peter and the apostles, that the prophets of old were true prophets, because their prophecies have been fulfilled. They said the Lord would come to His temple (Malachi 3:1), and He would remove all disaster from us (Zephaniah 3:18), and He has done so. The ministry of the prophets was proclamation before the fact. The ministry of the apostles is proclamation after the fact. **One great fact stands at the center of all history and of eternity—Jesus Christ is Lord! The prophets bow to Him from one side, and the apostles from the other.**

1. Describe the events in Zephaniah 1:1-13.

2. Compare the following passages.

Isaiah 13:9-16	
Joel 1:15-16	
Amos 5:18	
Zephaniah 1:14	

3. What good is trusting in wealth or possessions?   Zephaniah 1:18

4. What instructions and hope can be found in Zephaniah 2:3?

5. Fill in the blanks.

Through the ___________________________, God forms his people in the ___________________ of ___________________________, in the expectation of a new and ___________________ ___________________ intended for all, to be written on their ___________________. The prophets proclaim a radical ___________________ of the People of God, ___________________ from all their infidelities, a salvation which will include ______ the nations. Above all, the __________ and ___________ of the Lord will bear this ___________________. Such holy women as ___________________, Rebecca, ___________________, Miriam, ___________________, Hannah, ___________________, and Esther kept alive the hope of Israel's salvation. The purest figure among them is ___________________.   *CCC 64*

6. What two prophetic lines develop? *CCC 711*

7. Where do these prophetic lines converge? *CCC 711*

8. List all the passages in Zephaniah where you find the word "remnant."   How many?

9. Who does the Lord chastise in Zephaniah 3:3-4?

10. Describe the people mentioned in Zephaniah 3:12-13.

11. What will the Lord do?   Zephaniah 3:14-20

12. What does the Lord offer in Malachi 1:2, and what does He expect in Malachi 1:6?

13. Describe the sacrifices offered in Malachi 1:10-14.

14. What kind of offering does the Lord expect and why? Malachi 1:11

15. Where can you find a "pure offering?" *CCC 2643*

> The _______________________ contains and expresses _______________ forms of prayer: it is "the _____________ _____________________" of the whole _____________ of _________________________ to the _____________________ of ___________________________ and, according to the traditions of East and West, it is the "_________________ of _____________________." *CCC 2643*

16. Who is chastised in Malachi 2:1-9 and why?

17. What is the basis for human unity and brotherhood?   Malachi 2:10

18. Why is the Lord no longer accepting sacrifices or offerings?   Malachi 2:13-14

19. Compare the following verses.

Genesis 2:18-25	
Hosea 2:19-20	
Malachi 2:14-16	
Mark 10:2-9	
Ephesians 5:21-33	

20. For what did the prophets prepare God's people?

Seeing God's _______________ with Israel in the image of _____________________ and faithful _________________ _________________, the prophets prepared the Chosen People's conscience for a ____________ understanding of the _______________ and _________________ of marriage. The books of _____________________ and _________________ bear moving witness to an _____________ sense of marriage and to the _________________ and _________________ of spouses. Tradition has always seen in the _________________ of _________________ a _______________ expression of _____________________ _________________, insofar as it is a reflection of ___________ _____________—a love "_____________ as ___________" that "many waters _______________ _________________." ***CCC 1611***

21. What does God ask, and what does He promise in return in Malachi 3:10.

22. What will Elijah the prophet do?

More Books in the

COME AND SEE

Catholic Bible Study Series

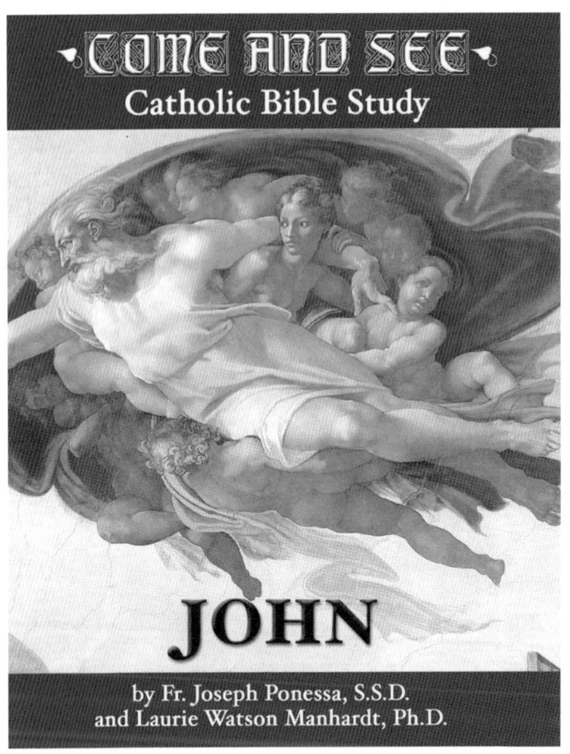

"Come and See"
Catholic Bible Study
The Gospel of St. John

21 chapters correspond to the Gospel chapters and takes 22 weeks to complete. Priced at just $19.95 + s/h. To order your copies today, call (800) 398-5470 or visit your local bookstore.

"Come and See"
Catholic Bible Study for Children
The Life of Jesus

This companion book to the adult study contains a Bible story, coloring book page for the child to color and a simple craft for the child to do with a little bit of help for just $14.95 +s/h

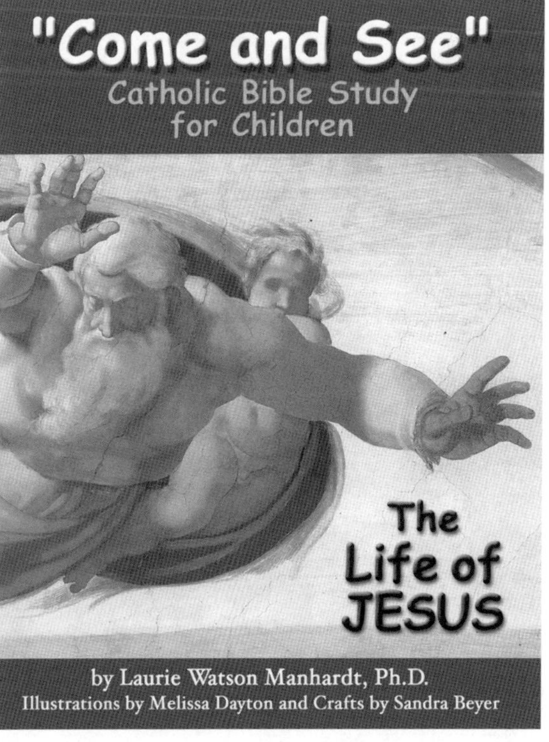

(tmore books on next page)

My Bible Study Small Group

NAME	PHONE	E-MAIL	PRAYER REQUESTS